Collected Early Poems of Robert Morgan

Collected Early Poems
of
Robert Morgan

Zirconia Poems
(1969)

Red Owl
(1972)

Land Diving
(1976)

Trunk & Thicket
(1978)

Press 53
Winston-Salem

Press 53, LLC
PO Box 30314
Winston-Salem, NC 27130

First Edition

CAROLINA CLASSICS EDITIONS

Cover art, "Mockingbird," Copyright © 1978 by Nancy Morgan
Used by permision of the artist

Cover design by Kevin Morgan Watson

Library of Congress Control Number
2024947274

ISBN 978-1-950413-88-1

This edition is dedicated to Jesse Graves

Contents

RED OWL: POEMS

I.

LAND DIVING

I.

II.

Trunk & Thicket

Part I

Part II

Part III

Introduction

Robert Morgan's welcome *Collected Early Poems* presents in one volume the contents of his first four full-length books, which appeared in steady succession over the course of a decade. His remarkable debut, *Zirconia Poems*, was published by Lillabulero Press in 1969, when he was only twenty-four. A limited edition chapbook titled *The Voice in the Crosshairs* was brought out by the Angelfish Press in 1971; nearly all those poems (joined with many more) soon saw wider distribution as part of *Red Owl*, released by W. W. Norton in 1972. In 1976, LSU Press published *Land Diving*, which gathered the first poems Morgan wrote after starting what would become a fifty-year career teaching at Cornell University. L'Epervier Press issued *Trunk & Thicket* in 1978; its author was still only thirty-three, an age by which Walt Whitman, Robert Frost, and Wallace Stevens had yet to produce their first volumes.

His publishers were based in Northwood, New Hampshire; Ithaca, New York; New York, New York; Baton Rouge, Louisiana; and Fort Collins, Colorado, respectively. Given Morgan's origin in and enduring connection to the mountains of western North Carolina, those places of publication seem worth noting. He has often been recognized as an important regional writer, but from the start he has found admiring readers far beyond the southern highlands. Asked in a questionnaire whether he considered himself a southern poet, he replied, "Since I was born and grew up in the southern mountains, and write mostly about the people, the land, the history of the region, it is inevitable that I be considered a southern poet, if I am considered at all. But the south is a part of the United States and part of the world. I also consider myself an American poet, and a poet of the planet Earth."[1] Those who first approach him out of a special interest in southern or Appalachian poetry soon realize that his work—early and otherwise—is poetry of the highest order, period, without regard to geographical boundaries.

Though his career has long flourished, most of the early books are currently out of print and may be difficult for some readers to find. Also, the representations of them in his two retrospectives—*Green*

---

1. See Michael McFee's "Seven Questions About Southern Poetry," in *Mississippi Quarterly*, vol. 58, no. 2, 2005, pp. 217-53.

River: New and Selected Poems (Wesleyan University Press, 1991) and *The Strange Attractor: New and Selected Poems* (LSU Press, 2004)—are only short samplings that insufficiently suggest the scope of his achievement by the late 1970s. The *Collected Early Poems* makes newly available many treasures withheld by those winnowings, including the extended performances of "Creek," "Flood," and the title poem of *Trunk & Thicket*, as well as that book's evocative prose interlude, "Homecoming." This omnibus edition restores easy access to a distinct phase of an essential oeuvre.

For interested readers, much insightful commentary is available: Fred Chappell, William Harmon, Mary C. Williams, Michael McFee, John Lang, Rebecca Godwin, and others have offered valuable analysis and context. Morgan himself has offered illuminating perspectives in his own essays and in interviews.[2] I think especially of two comments from "The Transfigured Body," a journal he kept in the early seventies. There he writes, "It is objectivity and precision that can be translated and that translates, the love of humble detail, a sensitivity to the eros of all things, focused recognition"; a few pages later, he declares, "I write to establish the reality of things. It's as if I'm afraid they aren't there unless substantiated by language, and consubstantiated." From beginning to end, this is a book of such recognition and sacramental transformation.

Asked in the same questionnaire, "What is the highest praise that could be given to a poet's work, southern or otherwise?" Morgan responded, "'You must read this.' The greatest honor is to be read." *Collected Early Poems* is a marvelous book, one that certainly deserves that highest praise.

—Robert M. West, co-editor of *Robert Morgan: Essays on the Life and Work*
Nov. 20, 2024

---

2. See, for instance, John Lang's *Six Poets from the Mountain South* (LSU Press, 2010); Jesse Graves and Randall Wilhelm's *Conversations with Robert Morgan* (University Press of Mississippi, 2019); Graves and my *Robert Morgan: Essays on the Life and Work* (McFarland, 2022); Rebecca Godwin's *Community Across Time: Robert Morgan's Words for Home* (West Virginia University Press, 2023), and Morgan's own *Good Measure: Essays, Interviews, and Notes on Poetry* (LSU Press, 1993), the source of the two quotations from "The Transfigured Body."

ZIRCONIA POEMS

for
Fred Chappell
and
(in memory)
Jessie Rehder

I.

Wolfgang of the Silences
or
Lakes Adrift in Mountains

High Country

In the hills, dead springs, blue flame of sky.
The horizon goes all the way around.

When it comes the darkness sprouts from rocks and fills
the valley. Splinters of ice form in the sky,
cold air stoking light.

A crystal trills at the bottom of a well
blasting tunnels upward.

It is the blue sun rising all night under the sea.

Close

The broom hill shines like a fox running.
Trees approach from the darkness and stand near my eyes,
fields lighting gradually.
In the moon polished sky stars crawl out
and press like spiders

deep inside a horse's eye.

Waking from a Dream I Think of Jessie Rehder

Lightning leaps like panthers through the trees.
I awaken from the long sleep floating
in my coffin.
The dark is heavy armor,
clear springs opening in air.

But it was you calling from the other side
of silence.

This slow leak into another
universe,
a hole appearing in our minds.

Waking Late in the Afternoon

An oak burns in the cold wind, sky of stained glass.
In the dream it was my death singing,
a blue sphinx lighting the sand reefs, the flowing savannahs.

I lay at the bottom of a lagoon,
my body a clock's hand turned by the current.

Rain, Drunk

Harpsichords beat a flamenco on the roof,
organ hum and flutter of the sea at my head.
The air is a bass string,
a coal of sound in the mind.

The rain splashes brief crowns on puddles.

Foxfire

Bright lace on the darkness grows
heavy as the meat of lightning bugs
crushed on bark, rotting leaves.

*

Flakes of the moon stuck to spongy logs.

*

Seconds sprinkled from a luminous dial on bearskin.

*

Glow worms crawl all night in stump water
without moving. St. Elmo's fire.
Foxfire swims like fish of the deepest troughs.

*

City lights seen from a bomber.

*

The eyes of dead wood stare like jack-o-lanterns
burning last year's sun
after a wet spell.

*

Coals of unlife,
chilly owls.

Night Puddle

The mist green moon rises only silences
away and grass on the ocean parts to let it pass upward
dragging chains through the cold waves.

Slips through a cobble of clouds, probing layers.
In the dark west clouds drift like ice in deep pools.

From a Cliff

Looking down through electric chairs of space.
Distance, a hot dry mouth, opens,
draws me to its roots
of frost. Winds the clock inside that yells, Jump,
crush the arms of gravity.

Very Old Man

Hounds bay in his breath,
face a wilderness, eyes like frozen fountains.
He speaks from a foreign country, words drunk
with exhaustion, wornout
habits of the tongue.
His shoulders are small as a child's.

Sits on the cold peak watching us climb,
or doesn't bother.

Elegy

Guess I'll light a rag out of here, he said
and blindness rose in his open eyes.

Tilted chessmen, tombstones graze on the hill,
drag shadows at the setting moon.
Eighty years go down

like a ship.

Cornstalks, Rainy Christmas

Wetting poplars, east wind stuns through the valley.
Cornstalks move like spiders running, black mold
spreading on shredded leaves, crowtorn ears.
Grains with the hearts eaten out by rats freeze in mud,
noon a long twilight.

The house aims only its highest window intact,
dustsoaked curtains sweeping the cold floor,
rooms mined with junk.
The pool on the hearth is soot.

A gray wind hones eaves and sucks at windows,
mnemonic shudder in the hemlocks scratching where an owl sleeps.
Wind bodies out the rain and pushes it in spells
on the porch, forces a crow to leap against the air
and let it carry him down the cornfields
and headon into night.

Passing Through

Cars approach on stilts of light and hiss
going past, steel beating air.

On back streets, dead wind.
Houses rise large as smoke through the trees,
oaks meshing in cold light.
Lawns are gray pelts, windows black as if holding water.

The distant surf of traffic quiets.
A manhole steams north. You could wait years for someone
to open a door, come home.

Driving

Converging on distance, I steer the opening air.
The highway, a graph on time, straightens constantly.
A bend turns the valley around,
engine hum soft as a powerline deep in the earth.

Cross a hill straight into the furnace door, sun welding
through pines, valley in sherry.
The ruby diffuses through the whole sky.

The highway flops north, settling out of mountains,
concrete stretched taut to night.

Swamp

The water is black as new tar,
mosstags plunging.
Stalactites touch into reflections and spiders run
pressing the surface.
Moccasins threading.
A bass breaks the long chord of stillness.

Water Tanks

The water tanks in South Carolina walk
like robots against the sky, bigger than the windmills
or firelookouts along the horizon
of filing black pines. Gray featureless heads rising
over factories and staring twenty miles through haze and over
mud cushioned creek bottoms
to another with another textile name for eyes
and mouth and lightning
needles thin as the radio transmitters to the north for ears
to hear the long overcast boredom
of Sundays, and cars going by and by and by.

They sneak around behind and follow
for miles, shrinking in the mirror to hot black pins,
old truck cabs looking down
on gullies and volcanoes of sawdust.
They rise like buds of junk out of kudzu,
high above the white wagonwheels at driveways.
The water tanks look on
like aluminum skulls, graffiti
hung from the mossy sky.

Lake Adrift in Mountains

After the speedboat, waves canter on rocks,
stroke like a hungry woman against the shore
and fall back, waning.

A pane of snowflakes falling away, weathered board mirror,
the lake spreads grain waves under the vodka air.
Chameleon water
duels the sky with silver.

Goosefleshed,
the lake is a field of bright leaves blowing, wings flapping.
Tight surface holding for miles.
The island is a rocky forehead watching.

A chord of wind, and reflections crumble.

The lake throws its flames at the sun,
fires in windows down valley.
Looking down where tall grass blows in the depths,
subterranean night.

Hunting

Waiting.
Quiet is repeated between twigfalls.
Lie flat in the fresh leaves watching oaks
vein the sky, black nerves
where a squirrel arcs the synapse between trees and gone,
leaves a forest twitching, mobiles.
Floating in the leaves.
Oaks are cockleburrs clinging to space.
Fall out through the limbs and keep going,
sky a blue lace on the gun barrel.
Wind turns the gold hickory, a forest flowing past.
The woods seem open as a cellar with the house gone.
Fallen leaves still smell of the sky.
A squirrel in the crotch, nervous, waving, grinding the shards
of a hickory nut. Blast
goes out opening interiors in stillness.
The huge drop of fur slides
off the limb and splashes to the leaves.
Gray hair and blood and leaves. Warm
in the pocket. Waiting.
Daytime moon white as doe's milk peers
through the spiders.

7:30 A. M.

Wind crawls like snakes through the truck cab.
Still wearing sleep we bounce down the haulroad to the site
and stand stiff as cactus
while the fire's made, warm till the boss comes.

Grab shovel handles slick with cold
and shovel
                    forty years.

In April the Air Is a Coral Sea

Blasts of forsythia, a bird drills the air.
Dark grass fills
the afternoon like water. Strange
glare of lushness.
Driving into the blue cave, the sky
is a huge drop of air, a wall retreating beyond pines.
Azaleas swim,
trees bending like coruscating bubbles
and the leaves are petals radiating green heat
from the gold in their veins.
I feel the glow on my face and skin.

II.

Creek

Creek

The spring is a lens
four feet across, focusing three wellheads to one stream.
Inside a lizard wrinkles, hill offering silver, quartz.
Here I anchor to the past,
drink from a dented cup and springs of two hundred years.

High country. The sky blows through grass and shrubs,
peaks like bare tundra.
Redbirds in the grass are leaves not yet brown.
Breaking in a curl of waterfall, the stream weights the valley.
The blackest boulder is a bear drinking
at the edge of sleep.

Meadows sag down from the treeline and pines
fang the high ridge, canyon falling away two thousand feet
to the old mill, dam cushioned with moss.
A flume shoots down through rhododendron to the pasture
where two granite tires lie abandoned.

Shot over rocks the current scoops a long pool
in the sand before rising pushing grit and minnows to the surface.
The pool is fish shaped,
tail flopping domes on the surface, scales of sunlight,
head biting at the foam and passing
it deep underneath where trout hang,
spoonfed by the current.
Worms leave trails in the clear eaves
and don't return, crawfish rowing out of sight.
The pool eats a river.
Rocks glide upstream dragging comets
of sand in their wakes.

After rain the creek is a candelabrum, green hills veined
by floods, the creek a bolt of water leaping
at and feeding the new sun.
Suddenly the trees are raining. Wind
sprinkles the air with a yawn.

In the shallows a tattoo of minnows,
leafswabs caught in the branches after floodtime.
Once I found the fetus of a deer wrapped on a rock in midstream.
Limp current, the creek sleeps here
for a mile before the rapids. Broke things on sandbars,
old fishing lines cobweb the bushes.

Sparkling from beyond the trees, a milkyway of sunlight.
Foxgrapes singe the air. A moccasin slides over moss and plunks
out of sight. In new school clothes
kids look for persimmons in the cold grass
where one flower trembles like a flake of sky.
Jewels shine like eggplants rotting.

Clear glass where it leaves rock
the waterfall glides in a half parabola sliding down air,
weight lost with fall.
Prows of mist lean over the gorge, through rainbows.

Bright subzero noon. Above the rag of clear water
rhododendron leaves are curled by cold, black folded wings.
Two hundred feet of hemlock slump in the white sun,
rabbit fur in wildcat droppings.
Cold blade of water thrashing rocks,
its muscle arching in a fin, sends dragon flies of light
into the pool where a trout beats,
frozen in the icy lens.

The valley winters under a range of hush.
You can hear a chainsaw miles away or maybe a woodpecker.
The white house sends out rays from bare oaks.
Willows sway like yaks walking, green fur
near the creek is rye.

Sprinkled with needles the snow is still intact in thickets,
blind cars rusting in the woods.
Pink clay stains through snow and yellow holes where rabbits pissed.
Cellars of air moving down creek.
The valley sails on, a farm in its hold.

III.

Zirconia Poems

Truck Driver

The road seems wide as a plateau
and from his tower of Benzedrine the world a kind machine.
Wife asleep somewhere, mind in second gear
he aims his windshield at the edge of space.
Myopic cars approach and pass.
The bricks in his stomach groan
and snow along the ditches sings in mint blue light,
tells him he's alone
except the voice in his mind and Night
which draws him on.

The Ballerina

Remember the Jewish ballerina who
a kitten in her thighs
and midnight purring in her eyes
commits the ultimate reality?

Or the afternoon when death
was fine as mink?

Theft

He waits until the lights are out and enters.
Elephants of darkness almost crush him.
He arranges the toys,
steals candy from the kitchen,
pilfers in the bedroom where the couple is sleeping.
The woman's rising breasts excite him
but he stops himself in time
and leaves at dawn by the window.
Flowers spring up in his tracks on the lawn.

Poem in Praise of Older Women

The tree is ready for the saw.
It sways against the sky and falls with grandeur
into waiting hands.
The house its body builds is large and warm.
Even the windows sing when opened.

Distances

Mind wanders down the long slope of trees
like small cat fur
turning blue in the midday sunlight of December
into a short valley
with only a cabin and a juniper
and one horse nibbling the dried grass
around an Indian grave.

Clear through the distance of memory
into the cabin where my great grandmother, a bride,
sits by the fire smoking her clay pipe
and watching through the door the gap in the mountains
where her man may come any moment
with gun on shoulder and quail swinging
and steps so rhythmic
they leave tracks in the mind.

Zirconia

Blue as mildew mountains break beyond the town
and shadows swim the valley.
Now filled with leaves the zircon mines
bleed dirt into the lake.
Further up, the millpond is a brain of mud
and high in the bones of a chestnut
crows watch the town
until the moon lights
the country like a TV screen.

Awakening

A stone is cracked open in the mountain pasture
and a thousand birds escape, imprisoned since the Ice Age.
Water strokes the silence of the air and falls
through valleys lined with fir.
The air above me sings a thousand miles.
I run along the icy streams and fall in darkness
where moments tick like dripping sleet above a campfire.
As far back as Wales
my family farmed the red clay hills of fear.

Wake

Staring through the lens of time the face
is whiter than the moon outside the cabin. A candle
pantomimes its story on the walls –
killed by his sons while sleeping.
Trees outside shiver, reaching for the dead man's ears.
The cabin soars upon the peak of stillness
and the mountains groan in wind,
disturb the sleepers by the fire who wander
through the dry leaves years ago
hunting deer and turkey.
And wind sucks at the high cave where the sons hide
waiting for the moon to die.

Prayer Meeting

A bonfire lights the faces, and the Greek
from Memphis sings and beats a tambourine, while his daughter
speaks in tongues, dances in the aisles.
Everyone screams, stamps, or waves
his handkerchief and cries.

Except the children who creep into the shadows
to watch, metal hardening in their eyes. A bitter honey
smears the wool of their minds.
Red salamanders crawl out of the moss. Their mothers
unpin their hair and reel with happiness.
The children watch, expressionless as blind men.

Key West Anniversary

I watch the sea translating
calmness into blue.
Through the doorway of a rainy day
I return to things.
Entering the half-life of love.

Dawn in New Hampshire

The lake steams like a hundred chimneys and firs
the color of moss enlace the lemon sun.
Later the sky dries
to petal smoothness and I find the moon fallen in the woods,
a mushroom, almost purple.

Durham, N. C.

A lung of smoke and cars
the city breathes at dusk a globe of haze.
Traffic swims like swollen eyes.

From the distance comes the cough
an old man carries in his hand around the world.

Long Beach

Far out surfers rise and die, soar beyond
the lace of foam like gulls, sea buckling under impact;
its tongues smooth and carve the sand.
Dune grass goosesteps under wind.
The ocean is a mountain range of water. The pier
crawls on its back like a centipede
and clouds eddy,
building sierras to the south.
I watch waves gnaw in the jewelry of light,
lunge in and crumble into feathers where the beach
shines like marble, honing the sea
to cut the dunes, retake a continent.

Beginning

Mollusks of snow behind cedars.
The darkness inside trees flows out, river
launching birds of fire.
The pools wear a skin of ice,
hold a leaf corpse near the surface.
A crow punctures distance.
After days of quiet
pines
roar their blackness at the fields.

Esprit Lucide

Walking out of a quiet house
after reading for hours
into the woods where snow is falling
is like waking into a dream.
The movement of the trees, my breathing,
the falling snow, are synchronized
and lucid.
I pass my hands through invisible cities of silence.
Everything is within reach
and the snow falls without a sound.

Spring Rain

The woman walks in darkness holding
breasts bare to the warm drops, her steps covered
by the splash on leaves.
As she steps through the arches of night
trees waken
with showers on her skin.
Twigs sway in the wind where her thighs ignite tremors.
Then the woods are left in darkness,
soft lightning in the trees.

Night Rain

Fearing something's been left outside, guilty that we're in,
we listen to the marching on the roof.
Turning like a herd of deer the river rises in fields of sleep.
The rain stings campfires, uncovers arrowheads,
and powerlines hum when wind
strokes water from the trees at dawn.

Waking at Night and Hearing Rain

The sweat that grows on corpses gleams like shattered glass.
A waterfall pours through the quiet
of a first snowfall
when I like to lie beneath the eaves
and catch the melting flakes in my eyes.
Just awakened in a cabin, rain falling outside,
someone beside me.

Storm

The rose of thunder broke like dry timbers
and petals fluttered on the windows.
Later the wind was a cold mouth; a muskrat
drew its net of ripples through the pond, and the moon,
bruised with blue,
floated to the surface of the pond.

Junkyard After Storm

Among the broom and rusting hoods,
dead radios.
Dripping goldenrod.
Thrust like thunder from the past
the tidal ring of Ringo Starr
floats
upon the nerves of summer.

Lightning falls like burning strings
into the trees,
steam rising from weeds.

RED OWL: POEMS

for Nancy

I.

Topsoil

Sun's heat collects in leaf crystals
crumbling.
Earth grinds the grain
to dark flour, drifts black flannel
over rock and clay.
Life invests
and draws on.
A lake rises over the world,
heaps of the rotting ocean.
Sun's heat adding
weight
piles on its light
century after century tarnishing
earth's metal.
Traffic of roots
hurrying. Places the raw meat
shows through torn to the quick.
Red clay mirrors.
Black fruit
growing around the earth, deepening
in the autumn
sun drifting down.

Cellar

The air moves as if something just left.
Snake breath.
Cool razors circulate
touching the skin with wet silk.
Breathing clear cheese.
Mold flowers grow like plastered snowballs
on the walls, rust-lacquered pipes.
The heads of translucent shoots crawl out of the potato bin
and run like wires to the window.
Once cut straight and firm
the walls have dripped and rotted to black jelly.
Jam grows blue fur.
The light bulb flickers as if circled by moths
fanning its coolness
and lighting on my neck.
Walls sweating mercury, straining
to the weight . . .

Woodpile

Chips surround the block
like foam
around a fountain
or bread scattered for the earth's fish,
packed in strata
for each winter survived
before rotting,
maple oak and apple,
fibers intertwining as they soak
into the ground, echoes
from each blow of the ax.

Well

A deep hoofmark left when the buildings are gone.
When you push away the vines
and look into the tower
an eye at the top watches you back.
Birds fly away
from a rock dropped in.
Here men and women drank from the earth
through a reed that held them by a tether
of thirst.
The well was a root they sunk
to maintain their hold here, a mineshaft
strong as the battlement of a buried city
for tapping the secret passages.
As you look the reflecting lens
imposes your silhouette on the stars.
This tree with its leaves of men
died from the top down.

Building a Dam

Two ways to make a pond.
Shovel a hole in the gravel under the stream
and let it fill (as it eventually will with silt)
or shovel up just enough mud
and rock to trap
the branch at a narrows,
to catch up a deep area of water
stretching around the bend,
up coves and tributary branches,
rising over weeds and cowtrails.
But after the dam is built, after you
throw a body of mud and clay
on the skeleton of brush
and tamp, covering
with turf,
and while the cold water
is rising every minute, extending
further back on itself and its feeders,
hushing the saults and covering muskrat slides,
there is the problem of a spillway.
Because no matter
how long delayed the stream
will reassert its motion and slice
a groove in the waterlogged turf and clay
or brush the whole project out of its way the first rain.

Windfall

Falling away from itself the oak
raises a helm of roots
steering it
back into the earth.

Bass

In the graveyard at the upper end of the lake
trees lie out from their stumps like shadows,
a log jam rising in late summer
bleached and knot-eyed.
Moss wigs.
Stumps clear the water
on roots. Blue gills flip
like coins at the surface. Minnows
sprinkling.
A tent of algae
is draped. In its shade
a hollow log is watching.

Rubies

Washed out where the stream unbraids
over mud and gravel (water selects
sand and leaves
the heavier fragments)
rubies wait
for a freshet to carry
them on. Each hard rain they descend
the valley a little and are buried
again, sometimes overgrown.
Weeds thrive,
their roots enclosing
insights, pieces broken
from the lurid brain inside
the mountain,
the beacon behind
the springs and up crevices,
bloodshot, aiming darkness. Aims
the terrible centuries
of heat and weight
into its perfect
structure,
its burning shattered
and worked out by the mountain's
lurching, scattered downvalley in separate
embers under moss, in mud.

Reach

Where the rockledge broke away
the huckleberry bush
has run its roots
out through a fissure
to the crevice and down several
yards past a hornet's nest
to another ledge
where slate chips have piled
like rotting leaves, and lichens and moss
have caught an inch or two of dirt.
Other roots have run back into the cliff
tapping the drip from rain
caught inside a mountaintop.
Thin roots have explored
all cracks
and grown like wedges
and slow charges of dynamite
prying off and disfiguring the cliff,
leaving their infiltration
exposed,
the support and supply
of the bush in jeopardy.
But succeeding in the long
drawn-out destruction to new land.

Resin

The pine is smeared with salves,
has thick scabs
and dripping sores.
The spinal fluid runs out
thickening a pouch around itself.
Reddish milk festers
from knotholes
hardening to quartz.
Boiled its spirits return
as oil, an intelligence,
colorless, volatile,
vehicle of color and solvent.
A whiff burns.
But the pine's sweet
blisters balm the air.

White Pines

Standing beneath huge pilings.
Up there where the sea broke, browsed along the sand
millions of years ago.
A faint surf breaks far overhead.

Wagon Roads

The wagon road was made by plowing around
the mountain with a moldboard
after the rocks had been pried out
and the main roots cut.
A furrow was plowed several times deep
and then leveled by dragpans
and shovels.
Rocks were tamped
into the branchbeds for a footing
under water and to prevent further erosion.
Rockslides and windfalls caused
the worst damage,
and thaw deflating the surface.
Low-hanging laurels had to be watched out for
and rattlers sunning on the rocks above.
The spring by the road had a can
on a stick.
The roads ran up high
to avoid marshes. But cars didn't follow
and they were left for logging and hunters,
drifting full of leaves.
When the trees are bare they wander
like trails etched by worms, unsure, getting lost
in coves, but always converging at gaps.

Muddy Road

Etching into permafrost
wheels slice through the suction of a hundred mouths
kneading and tearing off
as spokes tie knots
in the thick-lipped ruts.
The clay is so jagged it blisters
vision, like honey under a microscope.
Heaps of random carving and blottings. Wakes
fill and wash smooth.
The road quivers as a body
when jarred.
Now the earth itself is a lubricant,
squirms and squints bubbles
as a hoof sinks in
and pops out like a cork,
and the crater fills with old blood.
Treads are written over each other
and over yesterday's palimpsest of fossils.
Turds of subsoil are squeezed up.
Springs seep through
filling each track with warped sky.
Night, the road's history is set in stone.
Slashed grooves, puddles stranded.

Wire Grass

A star explosion, and the streamers, debris,
set off new stages where they touch
and are nailed down by roots.
To leap off again
skipping over ground.
Each new base fires out filaments
that overlap and dive under
the parent systems,
weaving a wire mat over
dirt, a web trapping sunlight
and area, not halting at water
but throwing its tendrils
across, floating
them out until they catch
or get washed back by the current.

Mound Builders

To place a bump on land, something
to rub the horizon, to climb
around and sit on
looking out over lakes and trees
level with the sun.
A place to walk spelunking
close to the black dirt where stars grow.
The mound rises to warn
intruders
and to last,
strewn with the bones of eaten animals
and oyster shells, and our bones.
The dirt is our ancestors.

Speaking

To roll rocks off mountains
you set them up like monuments and push.
They start out slow,
staggering, out of alignment,
but generate stability,
blurring over logs,
crashing, bobbing
up again like deer till out of sight.
And still you hear them running away all the way
to the bottom and stop, coinlike, in the leaves.

Thaw

Rods and cones
at the ends of fingers held up to the sun.
Snakes work in their roots of sleep
and dirt shows through
a huge fingerprint in the field.
Hiss of crystals breaking
as sun renders out the fat in snow
to run and be drawn to the sky again.

Slide

High on the mountain's gable
a raft of dirt loosened by the wet spell
tears away and spills
over
flattening the trees below
and bulldozing roots and boulders,
opens springs
in the mountain and spreads to the pasture.
Dirt squeezed high in the air
and packed for millions
of years crawls out
and pours.
For the mountain is burning down,
its tallow oozes to rest.

The Drained Lake

I walk into the fields like Noah
stepping again on dry land.
A fish swims off into the weeds for the first time.
The hills are draped in folds of mud.
I walk through damp valleys
crossing the ocean floor.
A stump is covered with old bass plugs
and carp rot in puddles.
Below the muddy fields and meadows
of stumps, a clear spring is running.

Land has risen from the sea again.
I follow the receding water,
climb wet dunes
looking for a place to build a city in the dark silt.
Already ferns of erosion grow into the hills
following springs to their source,
mining heaps and deposits
of topsoil and carrying them away,
black grease of rotten leaves.
Already the uplands are cracked and curling,
strewn with broken pottery; the paint
peels from old boards,
revealing sand.

We turn toward the desert,
cut down the trees and walk over them,
exposing the secret places, drain sloughs
and open springs to the drying wind.
This is the quest for extinction, translating
motion into landscape,
walking the clean bridge of sand
that falls through an hourglass building
a tiny mound of salt.

New-plowed Ground

Plow enters under dead weeds,
opens a seam to the creek.
With wings I could plow the sea.

        Curving black surf across the hill,
        blade shine on clods,
        foam of roots and stubble.
        You can't navigate without
        getting dirt in your shoes. Squeak
        of plowed-up field mice.

        Walk the rut it's easier,
        ground carved off a foot down.

Smell of water underground, cellars opened.
wormwet, cunt soft,
        washing toward rye.

Planting

Powder the furrow with salt
mined from the air. Wading dirt. Crushing soft clods
like strawberries.

        Corn—four to the hill
        Beans—one, white submarines traveling
        underground, lifting into the sun,
        birth of leaves from a bivalve.

Mining the hill with seeds,
green fountains splash in my tracks.
The earth a dark swamp, old hen settin
on seeds.

Sun leaves the dirt a brick
icecap.
        Briarshoals dying.

He Hoes Forever

Heat is a vacuum around the body filling with sweat.

Clods on the warped hill, chunks
of red brick and dying potato vines.
The fence wanders, rusty vines curling through weeds.
The pasture has filled to a lake of briars,
wave on wave of flowers rowing
where once the white horse ran.

He hoes the rocks, the afternoon, he hoes forever.
Cornpatch swung on the hill like a cape,
fields draped from the horizon,
clod tapestries.

The mountains wet blue tents watching.

Hog-wire Fence

Rust mortar still
holds a few bricks of air,
but the net seining others from
property and holding it in from the continuing
terrain is ruptured
and hard to find among the weeds
as a century-old deed in the courthouse.
Disappears turning over like a Möbius strip.
Runs through the middle of trees.
Otherwise the fence holds up
its rotting posts.
The tennis of ownership is played elsewhere.

Boredom

When the creek shifts intentions
and whips the other shore
scooping
a new pool with the weight
of its turn,
the backwater spins
to a stop and fills.
Silt falls out gentle as light snow
and the water clears itself
with no hope of moving on.
Sun sweetens the water with algae,
ropes of frog eggs.
The surface is plucked
by mosquitoes.
Land rises inside
and weeds grow out
to the new channel.
While the creek saws away saws away
only leaving.

Birling

The tree falls like a spoke turning into the hill,
drops and does a pushup
kicking back off the stump.
The chainsaw eats meat, bawls like a calf,
its tongue licking sunlight.
Dust rears a feather.
Held the ax
so long it hurts to let go.
Snaking logs down the groove.
They revolve in the pond nudging
and making room.
A wailing starts in the sawmill.

Ghost Tracks

Rolling up the carpet of snow in the yard
to make a snowman
we collect embossed chicken tracks
and tire treads made over
a month ago
by a rooster we killed for Christmas
and a tread already worn off, scattered like ashes
over the roads and smeared on pavements.
What we have is an almost perfect
replica while it lasts,
and as a great-aunt dying in January
said to her husband,
"You'll be married again before
my tracks are gone from the yard."
And he was.

Earthquake

A ghost dance of trees bowing,
breaking.
Pianos are launched like speedboats.
Hear the gods walking,
their tracks resonate like drums,
spreading in circles, dribbling basketballs in lockers.
Lovers lying face to face have the best
position for survival.
Gravity circles like wolves,
biting its tail.
One second the ground heaves
like a forest
then falls away to cliffs
at the world's edge.
There is no sacrifice to offer.
There is no sacrifice to offer.

Whippoorwill

The dead call at sundown from their places
on the mountain and down by the old mill.
They rise from the cellars of trees
and move up and down the valley
all night grazing like deer.
The call:
a rusty windmill creaks on the prairie.
Bats dipping and rising on ski jumps
are antennae
receiving and transmitting the code.
The whippoorwill interprets the news
from the dead, the unborn.

Exhaustion

The earth is our only bed, the deep
couch from which we cannot fall. Suddenly
the need to lie down.
The flesh will flow out in currents of decay,
a ditch where the weeds find dark treasure.

II.

Present

Our alchemy must be secret.
On cold moss
the redhot salamander.
Now is the dictionary of everything.
Doorway.
A place to stand.

Toolshed

The sticky smell of rust breaking out in blisters
after every wet spell and burning hoeblades, plows,
crowds the eaves with dryness and wets the lower air.
Dust is stuck to the greased singletree.
Wasp nests like gray sunflowers
hang from tin. The air here hasn't moved
in thirty years, old snow hovering above ground.
Pale weeds grow to cracks.
Half-eaten shovels lean on plows
caked with forty-year-old mud.
Dust drifts crossed by snake zags. Broken clevis.
Plow points are nailed like rusting leaves
to the rafters. Dauber combs dripping plaster.
A bird looks out of its nest in the corner like a dragon
lurking. 1936 license plate,
hames sucked weightless by dry rot.

House Burning

Came to see the house shine like quartz dilating
and spinning its facets in the sun,
so bright you can tell exactly where the flame
ends and the clear air begins.
Wood transfigures, a place leaving.
The fire gives X-ray vision
through the rooms
where boards sweat resin
and ribs and soaring rafters are wrapped
tightly in flames.
Came to see the bird catch fire
and fall into the basement where cartridges
go off in a close private war.
Hot air rushes out a hundred yards over
the faces of onlookers who came as to a hanging to see
the family sitting on a rescued sofa under
the apple trees watching
the fire preach its sermon over the pyre.
Ash circles like buzzards
in the smoke rising straight up before it scatters,
huge pencil scrawling on the sky.

Came to see the black cage of studs and rafters falling
in, the timbers of black feathers,
black satin crumbling
in sour clay to nurse unheard
of growth of crab grass.
The old folks living in a trailer around the hill,
the kids in ranch houses nearby.
Two chimneys facing above the cornfield.

Cedar

Smell the recorders buried here.
Music lies in the wood
as in the cat's entrails, in ore.
Faint musk of old arrows, canoe ribs.
Wood still giving
its breath, radioactive—releasing
a subtle verb for years
to fill whatever room or closet it lies in
till it's dark, inert
as the wood of cathedral carvings.
Weather leaches the glow
and withes of cool air plunder the fibers. The heat
is drunk off.
The wood reveals in lessening quanta the spice
from a country no one has seen,
leaking from a broken limb expanding to nonexistence.
But inside the scent's strong as light; it repels
the moth as two ends of a magnet
shun meeting.
For they are from the same country, the smell
lunar, musty, an ember so cool
you can hold it in your hand, and the moth
burning out of the dark, its semiquaver
weak as a photograph emerging in the darkroom pan.

Great-grandmother

Her skin like the gray paper of a hornet's nest
is frightening to touch.
As though you might receive a shock,
this close to the strange meat of death.

Chestnut

Opening a chestnut we find a huge eye
staring between whiskered lids.
This animal gone to extinction left
its eye to remind us
we're being watched
through the earth's dark lens.

Finding an Old Newspaper in the Woods

The sheets are exposed like film
photographing the gray and yellow seasons of decay.
The weather has flattened them to coarse
paper of leaves and pine needles.
They are almost dust.
The print has crawled off
and gone back to live with the ants.

Mendicant Rose

Alive on this tree of blood.
The bear snoring
in the heart breathes out
to the frontiers and pulls in again
as the ocean sends its roots
to the highest springs,
retrieving its gift.
A warm rain of blood falls on the slopes
and turns homeward,
spending its money all the way.
O mendicant rose.

Old Photograph

The glow from this tiny window, the distance
stuck to paper. The sunlight of seventy years ago selects
each wrinkle and thread of his coat, each whisker,
swells in the viscosity of her glasses.
Her breasts weigh on the brooch-gathered dress
like tallow pulling from a candle.
The house juts, each separate splinter of grass
aimed, carved in the old light.
Unpainted boards flare away from nails.
His bootstrap flops.
Sharp trees blowing.
They stare beyond as your eye
takes them again.
They stand at a threshold looking far behind you.

Copper

The meat of the sun is still pink inside.
But the skin's deceptive,
growing mossy barnacles
on bullets.
Drinks electricity.

Squeeze the juice out.
The lights are still on inside.
Molecules beating like pistons.
Hypnotic presence.
All metal is evil.

Stove

The fire whines its distant
siren and the stove door grins like a jack-o'-lantern
chewing its mouthful of flames.
The family gathers
like petals around the hot
black stem, bees returning.
Once a week the stove is cooled and polished
like leather, the flightdeck top
disassembled revealing
the depths the coals inhabit.
The stove is an extra digestive tract,
a vehicle for translating
the ancient vegetable
heat to the present.
Inside the fire runs its circuitry
and subroutines making split-level chemical
decisions.
The stove is motor.
Tobacco juice ferments in the bucket of ashes.
Later the heat returns and vanishes
through the coals.
The campfire dies while the hunters
are off hunting.
A sour wet silence pours down the stairwell.

Faucet

Water arrives from below
gargling in the long steel taproot.
Trickles gather
on the spigot's rim
and stretch away tangling.
A thin globe is blown
from the threaded lips
leaking
its knowledge
in tatters that form
perfect drops before hitting.
Bores out a solid auger.
Behaves
and misbehaves
surprising itself.
Water arrives blinking in the sun,
crawls away on the grass.

Bubble

The drop inflates like the spit
a glassblower speaks into, or you breathe
against the window till the pane
stretches out in a fluttering
sock and breaks off
healing
instantly to a perfect sphere.
Drifts wobbling out past the juniper.
Rainbows coil on the surface.
Wind distorts
the pneumatic toughness.
Encloses an embryo of space
beyond reach.
Glides spinning
into the grass and vanishes
to mist.

Church Pews

Under dust's upholstery
the wood itself still has the polish
of an apple,
the work of generations
of twisting children.
Salt is still in the grain
from afternoon singings and revivals.
The oil from sweating hands
and the rubbing of sweaty cloth
have left a finish
that sparkles
long after paint has cracked
and peeled, and in spite of the names carved
and figures drawn with pocketknives.
Only nailheads have rusted through the shine.
The pews are arranged like coffins
in a mausoleum.
It's like visiting an old courtroom
where you touch the wood expecting it to vibrate
with the voices of accuser and condemned.
The abandoned theater
will not perform.

Time

Snow-covered peaks gather in the north
like arabs talking.
You can't be sure you see them
but they leave an afterimage, detached
from the horizon, floating on haze.
Rugged seconds around the sky's dial.
If you look long enough they seem to march
like bishops shuffling toward hell.
I know the ground is a bridge
leading there—
to the white tents
and altitudes of death—
but I don't believe it. I don't
believe you can get there by just walking
the earth one step after another,
but must be snatched miraculously away,
fall upward into the terrible
blue emptiness.
When I stand in a field,
the field and I are a sundial.
But the body alone is a clock, and each
motion it makes.
Something must distract us, anything.
The cornfield slapping in the rhythm of a tennis game,
a crow flying his clockhands on a face
without surface.
The will always hungry.

Seismograph

Its hand goes on writing a letter
without stopping,
describes the ocean
throwing up shovels of water
like a gravedigger who never rests.
Hard to imagine
since we can only hold something
in mind by finding a corner or crack,
somewhere it stops and isn't.
Like thinking about death.

The ear's tiny seismograph is always writing,
but to understand
we must break up the account
into segments,
to hear the music.

Weed Above Snow

Folded like the meat of a walnut in sleep the worm
in his high minaret, the bulb on the weed stalk rocked by wind,
dreams of you thinking of him.
This poem the space between two mirrors.

Stump

You come upon a full basin, a level pool
of wood in which circles spread
imperceptibly
from the tiny seedling trapped inside.
Now that it's over we read a topographic map
of the tree's lifetime,
the concentric measures uneven,
stretched out
of shape by root dispersal,
only approximating the pattern
but succeeding
each other, counting
the years until the history breaks off.

III.

Red Owl

The sun is awake all night
flying unseen
through the earth searching
streams and caverns for prey, counting
the buried metals and feeding on blackness,
moist stenches, vapors of sleep.

She goes down herding light through crevices and roots,
through mud and the leaflike veins
where milk grows in the sleeping cows.

Rivers pour east to float her into view
and shadows lie down
for her rising, then travel across
to the next valley
on pilgrimage
to the ranges beyond her.

They are the eye's dream behind the light.

April 1970

"Buds crack like hatching eggs."

Each bears the sun's lush image
like a thumbprint.
I touch this leaf, this map
for the blind.

Bees Awater

You find one drinking at the creek,
scratching and drinking
before take-off.
He lifts back
and takes aim, firing homeward.
That's the moment to get your sighting,
get the direction and slant of climb
and you'll be looking right at the tree
on the ridge above
where the honey hangs inside
like cells of a battery
charged with sweetness.
The whole tree has the hum of a transformer.
Bees bubble, circling
like electrons.

Though excited as before a holdup
and hot from the long climb,
you drop the axe
and wait for dark.

2 A.M.

A dog barks through the horn of a valley.
Low moon burning in a cedar.
The creek mutters like an old woman
who walks in her sleep among the trees
dreaming of the life after death
when she will lie down like the stream
and flow to the darkness.

Meteor

A spike is driven in the air
so hard sparks fly.
I look up in time to see the meteor
losing its feathers
through the hourglass night,
as a hawk seizing its own death,
murderous for self-extinction.

Aspire

The breath of water leaves its body
frantic with ambition
toward the sun,
only to be frozen in the rare
altitudes and abandoned by the light,
to gather and begin the long fall
back to itself,
to the slavery of carrying
the earth's debris.
Yet sure as Avogadro's number
it rises, purified by the journey.

Power

The stream trots like an immortal dog on the wheel,
varies its pace only with flood and drought,
searching for the earth's center.
Not even stopping at walls
but climbing on its own shoulders over.
For the sun lifts up a great counterweight
of ocean that falls
pressing everything to motion,
stretching twigs on the forests of mines.
And the earth reverses the weights automatically.

Even the little spring here is compelled,
raises its head striking,
pulls on its roots,
cannot lie still.

Wind

Spirits revive, return from their journeys.
You step into the thrust of music,
lean into a great voice, the long muscular syllable.
We are thirsty for the wind
carrying its mirage, the great door closing
and closing far off with a sonic boom.
The air is off balance,
falling over and over itself like an avalanche
of leaves. Lightning rides the ridge
hurling its lasso.
The long shout drives it to its nests.
A cave unfurls like a parachute behind me,
follows, a clear shadow
pushing like a candle as the darkness
inside tries to soak through.

Warm Winter Day

Pines rise like shadows aimed north of the sun,
rivers shining down oaks.
I relax to the ground looking
into space (the great blue seed) like an exile
turning homeward.
An acorn lies near my eye, long brown breast.
The sun is a spring feeding
the wide blue valley.
Whiskers and spokes of fire twist across the distance
like a rope bridge in Asia.
The black hole behind the sun
hurls its dungeons.
You must go into the wilderness alone.

Day Lilies

The sudden appearance on roadbanks and along
ditches, in weeds where nothing has been seen.
Each stretching to get a look,
returned
the color of a salmon
to the spot its parent marked for a day,
risen from the dark by searching
root deltas,
the red climbing headwaters
to burst the stem's thermometer.
By trails and isolated meadows, speckled
in the updrafts,
each jumping
clitoris of color.
Meditating like Tibetan monks,
tracking the sun.
Tonight they roll up like cigars.
As wind returns they rock
the earth, make it pitch and run.

The Spring

Kneel and look into the quiet
hermetic valley, desert of broken armor,
sand beacons.
The breath of underground islands lifts to the sun.
Horizon feeds
on the dark hill of space
where the dead go.
Smoke of extinct tribes in quartz.

Light Is Bleached

Light is bleached by dust and insects
torture space, creak like rusty springs in the grass
where the sprinkler swings
a rope of water on the lawn
and last greens echo drowning under
yellow, and mud is sharpened by the sun.

The arches of the mole are cracked by drought.
Drugged by cold insects gather to the warmth of boulders,
pokeweed dripping berries.
The lake aims a totem of reflections at the red maple.
Squeezed like beads of oil from the hard ground
ants march south.

Dirt piled by ditches is still warm, heavy tents
settling as the sun draws through pines
dripping strings of honey.

Flocks of yellow fly from the poplar.

Rabbit Tobacco

Seeking magic, the journey,
children collect and hoard the earlike leaves
for smoking in attics and cedar groves,
lighting the fuse of adolescence.
Fire's rapid decay exhilarates,
lungs eat vegetation's death.
The spark swells
like a track in melting snow
to cover the leaf,
and the ashes are scattered carefully.

Bonfire

I say the book flutters its pages like a nugget
(fountain peeling itself)
of excited air
remembering the magma.

Milk Gap

Climbing up into the gap between day and evening,
to the saddle of trampled dirt,
to meet the stock
halfway coming down
from the ridges and balds.
Their tinkling closes in from hollows
and rides downdrafts.
Hogs burst
from the undergrowth
heavy with roots and acorns,
come for a few scraps.
The young bull dominates to the shuck rack.
Cows hook to get a position, banging
the brass flowers on their necks.
Their calves feed from behind.
Sun takes aim
through here.
Throw down the stool
and milk quickly. The cow turns
to watch her strange calf.
The voice of the bucket
hushes as it fills.

Cold

Chicken droppings chalk the yard and boot tracks
are soled with ice.
Bright as the light in a rose clouds lean, converging on the west.
Hay and sorghum breath of cattle eating
warms the loft where wind cuts like rays through cracks.
Snow on the northern slopes losing its voice as the sun goes down.
The yard is a floe of wind which I must swim going home,
ruts freezing leathery, then stone.

Hubcaps

The tractor runs over dirt and shapes it, turning
stubble and moving the hill
furrow by furrow to the terraces,
slicing clods, wearing
them away and chopping roots
to rot in sweet beds of decay.

The owl: eyes like arenas
gathering
the weeds and hungry ditches.
She guards the air like a monument
shedding a field of energy downwind.

Old hubcaps burning all night in the creek.

LAND DIVING

for my mother and father

I.

Dark Corner

Steep

Driven out from the centers of population,
displaced from villages and crossroads and too poor
to acquire the alluvial bottomlands,
the carbon-dark fields along the creek,

forced back on the rocky slopes above branches,
to the flanks near the headwaters,
pushed to the final mountain wall, I brace
my faculties against falling out of labor

and prop up or stake down every stalk, dig
terraces and drive fences to save what little
topsoil there is from the gullywashers
hitting almost every afternoon up here in summer.

Cow trails babel the steepest knobs, make
by spiral and switchback the sheer peaks
and outcroppings accessible. I plant only root
vegetables, turnips, potatoes, and prehensile creepers.

Too far to carry whole or raw things
into town, I take the trouble only with something
boiled down, distilled, and clear new
ground every three or four years.

I live high on the hogback near
dividing water, I disaffiliate and secede.
I grow ginseng in hollows unlit as the dark
side of the moon, and confederate with moisture and

insular height to bring summit orchards
to bear. I husband the scartissue of erosion.

Affliction

On the slopes where the old
blighted years ago,
new
chestnuts sprout and
thrive until the age of saplings, then
blossom and die.

How the old roots keep sending
shoots every spring
hoping the canker's gone.
How the buried sap must
remember the sun and
former height, keeping the veins

stoked winter after winter below
the frost-line, always raising a new stalk
like a periscope to find
if the poison has subsided, tasting
sweet wind off the
ridges and refueling on light,

after decades still trying to break through
and establish hold,
watching the new pumped by
hoarded sugars
and thrilled by the open
reach puberty, almost produce and

fertilize a seed before the curse
strikes the species back
into its dungeons.
Like us straining to ascend
immortal
only in dirt.

Double Springs

I used to wonder how
two springs could issue from the hill
a yard apart. Why not dig deeper
and unite their flow?

And later realized they
surfaced close from opposite
directions. The southern
sweeter, though the northern's steady

effluence came cold, even in the dry
months when its neighbor
slacked and almost stood, with
algae thickening the edges.

In the church nearby I've heard
sermons on the trinity describe
their separate currents merging to
one branch. The sweet uneven

head rose from the hillside leaning toward
Dark Corner, while the constant
icy thread emerged
from the farm country. In summer

they condemned the slow one and
when I came down to drink before
or after preaching its partner sure
enough ran clear, with ebullition

dimpling the surface above the pores,
and purifying lizards gripped
the sandy floor. But after swilling
there I'd dip the gourd

into the slightly silty left
embellished now with leaves and spiders
and aquatic mosses for a richer sip.
That ungodly taste I'd carry home.

Signs

No fishing on Sunday
we crayoned on the plank above
the Lemmons Hole. At six or seven
I knew wetting a line then
would bait electric eels
that send underwater lightning
up the string
to kill the guilty angler
key or no.
The cowtrails came down into
the shallows of the pool
and for all I knew continued
to a fata morgana pasture of cocoons
below. Swimmers on the sabbath
would be taken by the suckholes
and whirlpools down into
the sinks of filth.
Don't play with BB guns on
the Lord's Day or a pellet will
ricochet into an eyeball.
You follow a girl into the brush
along the creek after church
a cloudburst may wash
you out still coupled and naked
onto the sandbar
where they have baptizings.
Trash backs into the central
eddy and queues like a moccasin
coiling where the Cochran boy went down.
Current galls on rocks around the bend
where they found Grover
frozen with his bottle.

Going Barefoot

Sure I've seen kids walk to school
barefoot in the snow and stop
to warm their feet in the branch.
But every year the first of May
regardless of the weather we
took our shoes off religiously
and put tender feet on the new grass.
And even when it came late frost
or chilling rain we never put them on again
until the first of October.
I have walked with a stubbed toe
swollen and runny as a rotten potato
in the dew that gives blood poisoning
to turn the cows out.
By June I ran on callous sandals
down the gravel road
and teased copperheads among the weeds
looking for berries.
A tourist lady once paid a quarter
for her kids to see me skip
along the rocks.

I have gone barefoot into the creek
and into the snakey thicket above the falls.
Loitering discalced along the platform
of the market I stepped on
a burning cigarette, and stood
with naked soles on the hot pavement
before the courthouse.
My heels have been tarred by runny
highways and stuck to manure
and wormy mud. I have worn
socks of sweat and dust in the cornfields
and wiggled my insteps into the cool
underdirt for comfort.
I have stepped on nails and
barbed wire and glass in the leaves,

and stood vulnerable in the presence
of tetanus and hookworm.
Nettles plowed into the baulk
have left arrows in my arch.
I have put a toe in mousetraps in
dark corners of the attic.

Easter Algae

The first warm day in April patches
swollen by the sun tear
from the pond floor where they've stuck
all winter coating the mud and rear
to the surface like leaves bucking
and shedding silt. Gather in thick

huddles downwind black as grease and clotting
against the leeshore. Under
the slick every drop is busy
as time's square. I saunter along
the rim and slaughter of last year's
cattails, feel the unknotting

and polymering amorphous as graphite
cells, surprised as a child
finding rabbit eggs in weeds at
the old impossible blessedness
in the royalling water where fish seeds
wink like new genes in the sky.

Concert

When Aunt Wessie played she
reached into the keys with heavy
arms as though rooting tomato
slips, sinking hands in to

the wrists and raking the dirt
smooth, humming as she worked.
Would awaken suddenly from her reverie
and plunge onto the keyboard jamming the

pedal in like an accelerator
and slapping chords over
the melody till
the whole room filled

and beat like a sounding board
and every note on the trellis of wires blurred.
Almost blind, she stayed alone
in her house on the mountain

while we worked off in the fields.
As her hearing failed
the TV blasted soap tragedy
all over the valley.

Roost Tree

Too wild or many to use the coop
behind his house my uncle's chickens
gathered near sundown close
to an old arborvitae,
still pecking, a few
maybe dusting in the potholes
on the bank.
One by one they'd flap
up into the branches until
the yard was empty and
the waterpans full
of evening sky.
Squawking over favorite
perches and jarring
limbs they shifted like
berries of an abacus on tiers
of hierarchy,
rooster high in the steeple.
They loaded that old tree
of life miserably,
thirty or forty
whitewashing the trunk
and lower limbs, dripping
even on each other.
The bark they polished
dusty with mites, leafage threadbare.
They settle into dusk clucking;
one flutters down for a last
blade or worm and then back—
disturbing neighbors to
reassert preference.
Frightened by a dog or
possum in the night they
raise a half-hour fuss.
The rooster crows by three.
Sometimes a hen gets heated in her
dream and lets an egg

go, bursting on the limbs
or ground like too-ripe fruit.
The fox may lick its
splatter,
but cannot climb.

Cold Friday

My grandfather would say the arctic
camphor breathed on the mountains
that day dry-rotting flesh.
Back in the '90s whilom. He
drove a team down the frozen
creek to mill and saw where Searcy's
cabin burned the night before.
No snow, but scraps
of ground raised on silver
hair as if pulled out by
the near vacuum.
As if something big had left,
the valley ached with stillness.
The wheel was locked
by its beard to the creek.
Stopping by Orr's at noon he heard
the chickens never left the roost
but stayed on their perches like hoot owls
through the gloomy morning.
The callous sky and hungry air
drained his muscles
on the steep trail.
The buckets had welded to
the floors of stalls.
A wide absence drew from the ground
and chimneys every calorie, reached
into burrows and up the deep
hollows where deer
huddled in their yards.
The churchbell cracked and
bulbs in furrows detonated at the core.
The spring shrank under a shield
protecting its sources.
The parasitic emptiness
fed at crevices in rocks
and cabins. Such
poverty of the elements

and splintering failure of
the poplars by the creek
took away speech where they
tightened to the fireplace.
Frost crawled on their backs
threatening to bite.
They prayed for the black
panther night to be lifted. One
asked to see the trapdoor of hell
opened as less painful
than flesh setting like tallow.
White spores cultured inside the windows.

Sproutlands

Now the great warriors are recumbent in weeds
or molder down the hollow
in a seance of water.
The stumps have bled wet tables of sugar
for years drowning flies and yellow
jackets, foaming like tankards

in warm rain. The wide platforms
of the titans crack their
rings and blacken
though we still read their methuselan
circumference where
they scatter like bases of a game.

The children gather on the rims sucking
on the old incredibly extensive
root systems and spurting on the ancestral
sap three times faster than all
seed growth. They put out leaves
enormous and lush from skinny

stems and crowd each other
into starvation. For years these
hinterslopes and clear-cut pinnacles will
wash away and chap in rubble,
bandaged only by brush and weeds.
Until immigrants and the rare

hardy scions reforest and reshade
them, for all the setbacks straight,
though less tough
for lack of competition. Of
the graveyards of the giants no trace
except likeness in the young leafage.

Getting Out Rock

Wading into the shallows my father
wore the rock like an apron
streaming creek water, choosing

among the polished spill of
rubble the right thickness every time
for a homewall, completing already in

his mind the puzzle these fragments
would compose, selecting as for a
quilt contrasting surfaces, quartz

and peppery granite, and heaving from
their cool sockets and settings to dry
stacked within reach of the wagon

like coins and chips of his stakes.
To raise back up the mountain they
broke from and shoulder them

in place like jewels of a mosaic
thrown on the turning seasons, a creekbed
he wrapped around the family.

Surveying

The new-sold mountain down by Willow
will have its facets cut
and polished by the dozer,
and through the transit lens new
lines will be shot
and inked right over

its saplings. They'll pin
acreage to the flanks
and triangulate the ledges,
ironing flat the edges
of the hollow nussing rank
swampland at the foot, within

sight of Refuge Baptist Church.
With one blow of his light
hammer
the tongues-speaking auctioneer
transforms to rubble. It's the sight
of the still-wooded ridge that hurts.

After Church

Coming out of the damp sanctuary
a permanence flared in the pine
grove, and ice signaled from the
dormer cliffs and from

the snow Lhasas on Pinnacle.
Even the black coverts of laurel
and bleached pastures said
something comforting. And the dead

fields welcomed me to their exposures
after the swaddling word. What
could be more everlasting
than chickens scratching the manure

pile and the cold catalog in the toilet?
The wilderness lunged widdershins
moting the sky's perfection
and the sky fell nondenominationally at

nails feasting, as they had for
half a century,
on the wood of the
dilapidating fence corner.

Face

The story went that once someone, an unbeliever,
looking into the clouds saw among the luminous
caravan of shapes and smokes, the usual sheep

and outcroppings of battlevapor, signals, choo-
choos, stretching fish, when suddenly in
one great chunk of the sky the Lamb himself,

the face of longhaired Jesus, looked sadly down
at him. Struck down on his way from that moment
he believed. Having a camera he snapped the

quickly dissolving icon. Advertised on radio
and at revivals that photo sold thousands. Looking
at the black and white you never found the image

at first, but when it came rushing out of the
wisps and puffs hardening into a perfect likeness
the recognition was beyond all expectation chilling.

For months I kept eyes ahead or to the ground out
of horror, feared looking back I would see
the Tiger clawing through eastern azure.

Dark Corner

Was said around home nobody
lived in Dark Corner, just
near it. For us it was across
the ridge in South Carolina.
After dark with the wind right
you could tell somebody was making.
Strong as the fermenting shade
under an appletree
fumes came chimneying
through the gap in Painter
Mountain. Whole cornfields asweat
through an eye. What focus!
Not to mention sunlight gathered from the hillsides
by the flush of cornleaves, and ground water
freighting minerals taken by sucker
roots, long weeks of play
with hoe and cultivator before
the laying by; stalks stretching
exhilarate in the July night
till sun fills the cobs' teeth
with oil. No mention
of top cutting,
fodder pulling. Talk
of digestion in mash vats at the head
of the holler, sugar agitations,
transubstantiations, work
of bacterial excitements till
hot sweetness arrives. Comes the runoff
calling from the corruptions and burning
a ghost returned by the reflector
to a cool point. Manifests
heavy drops, pore
runny with lunar ink.

Back up under the summit line
where smoke is hid by haze
and updrafts lift
the mash smell a few
hundred yards out of state,
the lookout waits on the laurel ledge,
gun in lap to fire warning.
A rattler suns near, his crevice
high over the settlement.
Down there houses propped, a toilet
wades the creek on stilts. Man
here'll go down
on his daughter, god
damn her soul.

Uncle got sent up for moonshine,
did time in the Atlanta pen.
Long as water runs and corn grows green
and fire boils water I'll be making,
Judge, reckon on it, he said.
But something there broke him.
Rumor blamed the whippings. He
came back old, a new man.

Turpentine the Dog

Catch the stray dog hanging round,
that howls all night
and quaffs our eggs,
that chases the cows into the hedge
to scratch their udders and heat
the milk with adrenaline.

Drag him away down to the barn
and tie to the crib
while you soak a cob in turpentine.
The lift the tail, undoing the line,
and jab
the vaporing nubbin up his ass. He tears

away and jerks as though
trying to swallow air
into his behind --
and yelping rolls in the cool vines
along the branch. With a holler
drags haunches over

the grass, and lights out again.
You'll hear him bellowing
from time to time across the valley,
a squeal coming when he
thrashes in the creek and water stings
the burn, and last on the horizon

as he dives for South Carolina;
he won't be back.
I've heard of dogs lived seven years
after a turpentine but never
showing near the place they go struck
with religion and spoke in tongues.

Flood

How much the rain outside my window
this morning looks like a loom
strung with electric
warps through which the robin
darts and returns wefting
a fabric of summer,
knitting roots and new
borders on leaves; he
unties knotted worms
from the selvage grass
letting the full cloth blow
away and soak out of sight even
as it's woven. Now,
staff and distaff, the
rainspider has thrown
his web over the sun.

Drops slide along the twigs of the shadbush,
shift and cohere, separate and
drop off. Line up at a joint
queuing to jump
like paratroopers;
the load of drops remains
constant till long after
the rain is over.

A green floating scum
collects in eddies
of ditchwater,
almost the pure
snot of life itself,
digesting heat, boils
in pools structureless, a blur
previous to form.
Bits catch and wisp off rocks,
stream away bright
polymers, constructing

colossal molecules;
fills backwaters with
green sperm.

A whole cloud fails out
on the acreage of the summit
stampeding to ditches,
filling depressions and

mounting terraces, spins
trees loose as it comes
down collecting everything.
Water needles down

scratching the grooves,
sets a farm pond free and plows
open a beaver swamp.
The creek valley is defecated.

Bridges heave
bucking away, a herd of
logs crowds into the bend.
The creek fans out over the bottoms

and fences of stubble
slowed by area, stands for
a few hours waiting to spray out
the slot in the valley' lower

end. By the foothills it
hardly stirs the river's pulse,
clouds the swamps lightly. Logs rot
in the first lake's backwaters.

Go far enough upriver to cut in
so the current runs out
at the field's upper edge.
After the gate's thrown, melt
from the glacier meadows
and runoff of the high lakes come
proving every turn and drop
of the ditch, turning
loose on the field and filling
each depression and trough to
the lower end. Starts
sweeping back generally
over the ground swamping the seedriddled
ridges and soaking down to subsoil.
Water treats the powdery loam
with a transfusion,
like the introduction of a hormone
flipping switches. Just
when the ground's full and
before it gets watersick or the
oxygen leached, the gate's
closed and the flooded
land drains up into the sun.

Where a sheet of water lay
on the field two weeks,
weeds blacken as though electrocuted
up to the floodmark.

There is the stench of wires shorting
out, hair singed. Wind fuels
itself on the bubonic mud
of a battlefield. Poplar roots are sore.

Waterbruised stems and leaves
slicken, smuts take on
the bushes and scalded saplings.
Leaves of the wild cherry

whose roots lay under the clear
sheet of water
cure yellow and
fallout across the rubble.

Because the forests and absorbent turfs have
been stripped off, because we build
too close to the moving water,
we protect ourselves against all excess,
domesticating whole rivers and watersheds;

empty or near-empty reservoirs wait in the mountains
with gates open and weedgrown basins for
the heavy rains or thaws, reserves of
volume serving negatively like the spare tanks
a camel draws on far from the oasis.

The more regulation the more we fear
extremes and overflow, the sudden wash
down gully and branch spreading out over cultivation,
tearing chunks from the banks and eroding
new channels. Fronting the river from where it

disperses into the gulf running back up
the deltas and boll to the tributaries and up each
of them to the foothills, and sometimes within
sight of the mountains, you see along the bank
and often miles over the marshes

and forested floodplain the embankments, the
fortification running on the land like a swollen
vein now grown over with brush and saplings, already
assimilated by the terrain, raised along through the low
country like some Chinese wall against the current

from the north, against an invasion of the deadly
overplus and its gift of silt like blood on
the altar. Our ramparts let water run higher than the city
it cuts through, waves sloshing on walls and fish
nudging the shore ahead. How they wait miles away

from the current through dry autumns and cold
nights. And closer in another policy to impound
and preserve, the cobbled banks and bed, the masonry
and revetments to starve the river of sand for
gnawing its meanders. Seawalls of boulders and pilings

train the flow. How we stick to the bluffs and far
back elevations, leave the rich low-lying flatlands
to reeds and swampoaks, leave a buffer to
trap and stretch to exhaustion the rebelling channels,
thin and dissipate the lethal thrusts, dampen the

amplitude of snake dancing, pull taut the
oxbow tangles, wall off where water would insinuate,
ride herd on the curriculum.

The falls milks over the rim fusing
to a central core losing
weight all the way

down to the first ledge it
marks by flaring off. Welds
spewing from the boulders whitehot.

In the arclight wrestles, plunging
a deep root into the earth. And
still at the top water spreads thinning

to the edge and tears
off a sheet sliding over, striking
wings on a rock wading in the powder.

The new water fails flattening out to
smooth the cantankerous shoreline,
but sluices

and sprouts a cold two-pronged
thrust clearing out in a long
filament reeled by the sun.

At Fundy waves come in off the Atlantic
into a long bay that narrowing traps like
a funnel or loading chute
the sweeping weight
of the ocean crowding down
the shrinking corridor.

Waves forced to climb on the back of
waves are squeezed tall above
sea level and rammed through the closing fjord
as the separate currents and lunges
resolve into one great vector
riding victorious up the canyon

to a glassy peak at the bay's head and
holding siege while
the pyramid of arriving tides
weakens and the deep pulls back its support
leaving the assault to fall away
and slide off layer by layer down

the firth. Villages
constructed near this extreme
are stranded across miles
of the oozing tidelands.

Yes, impossible not to believe that if
we paddle against the muscular current far
enough, survive the fever and mosquitoes
of the marshes, the Indians encamped on
bluffs, make the great portage past the falls
reaching foothills by late summer, living on
buffalo shot from the banks and waterfowl nesting
in the shallows, Yes, we'll enter the long
gorge curving back to the snowcaps, and
wrestling the clear thrust of creekwater,
come to the final branch and its ultimate
pool. Yes, we can get out there and carry
over the alpine meadows and thaw runlets of the
col across the Divide. There! Yes, just over
there the Great River of the West rises descending
with ease out onto the floodplain, and gathering
in one long sweep through savannahs, past orchards
and grape-heavy trees, brushes away snags
and sandbars to the open sea, and beyond
the tropical scented, wisdom-lighted
islands of the welcoming orient. Yes.

II.

Land Diving

Horse Shoe, NC

Little town by the river
I nail you up in my memory
for good luck far from home,
as an emblem
I pass under hardly
noticing you're so constant
and everyday
there in the crook of the French Broad's arm,
in the frog marshes.
And I like to pick up and play
with you, toss you around
trying to score
on the peg of meaning out
here in the vast and traveling
world.

Voice

Creating shadows and dopplers
of obstruction the
pine filters song from the wind,
slices music from the open
flow causing air
to reflect and refract against itself.
But a greater resonance is
made by tying off
a knot of its motion in an eddy,
a swirl inside the mouth of bottle or cave,
filling and inflating
the belly
neck and lips.
And the urn or skull,
egg or hollow tree, glows
with sound
though broken and empty.

Land Diving

Though it's no disgrace refusing
some things must be done.
And present accomplishment
is no guarantee
of future.
You must come close
as possible without touching
to prove brinksmanship, fly
from the sapling girdered tower
before the whole village, leaping with a scream
against the wall of fear, step onto
the white-hot floor
of emptiness
holding only to yourself.
You will know the pure isolation of fall.
The vines bound to your feet must not snag
on the scaffolding
or they will swing you crushing
into the frame and braces.
They must not break
or be an inch too long
or you will be smothered by
the swat of earth.
Yet the meaning is the closeness.
No stretching out your arms;
you must be jerked to a stop face against
the trampled dirt
by the carefully measured
bonds.
Only they can save you.

Plowing Snow Under

Mold has grown on the field overnight.
Time to crank up the tractor
and plow under
the yeast-rich slickness,
reversing the sheet of new white
topsoil thread by thread.
The pure insulation
is ripped off and crushed
under mud,
soaks in like the dirt's shadow,
crystals and crumbs
of white manure
smeared in
to buoy and shoot the ground
through with nitrogen.
Swelling the dough at thaw,
pushing up drifts of lush green.

Feed Room

Dark except strips of light through cracks.
Walls loaded with harness.
The floor is a rich
sprinkle of feed dirt.
Rats crackle behind the sacks.
Reaching into the meal bin
the musty sides smother, but deep in
the crushing is warm
as a banked fire.
Don't cough in the barrel.
The cottonseed meal's fine
as snuff.
Vats of bonemeal, laying mash, nubbins.
Sweet dust of molasses
in dairy feed.
Bags of mixes, shorts
and sweetfeed.
Dust cultures on glass.
Panes of light like aquariums.
A dirty china egg lies on the shelf.

Hogpen

In the pine woods, at the log
enclosure with a roof
over one corner,
you can get up close
to the grunting breather.
And he knows you're there, always
watching through a chink.
Suddenly whirls
his great weight
squealing to the other
side, for all his size quick
as a cat; stands
in mud plush.
Living out
our exile we come
with offerings
of scraps, bran.
Slipped over and gomming
his snout he's after
it so fast, snorkeling
under, coughing.
Licks the trough bare to
meal stuck in cracks,
clabber whitening
hoofpools.
Sun brews the
tincture, flies steaming.
A scree of cobs bleaches downhill
where canfuls of worms can
be dug every foot.
It's a good place to play on
a hot day, in the pines,
spice of needles,
resin swelling.
Play close to the slow
talker
panting behind the logs.

He listens, taking
an interest.
Stirs in the inner
chambers, blessing the hours.

Headlights

To be caught in headlights walking
the dark road seeing with
feet and body
alone
and suddenly hit
by the flame thrower,
vision splintered and nailed.
You are naked to the light's interrogation,
awakened on the stage, photographed,
stunned like the deer.
Shadows stream away
pulling at your feet.
Someone flicks a cigarette
sparking fuse.
Your first thought is
to jump over the bank and hide.
Only pride keeps you walking ahead
fighting. And you are left
blinded,
stepping through walls
of dark rubble.

Pumpkin

By fall the vines have crawled out
twenty yards from the hill
coiling under weeds.
The great cloth leaves have shriveled
and fallen. No sign of a harvest.
No way to tell where the pumpkins are scattered
except wade into the briars and matted grass,
among hornet nests and snakes,
parting the brush
with a hoe. Or wait
a few weeks longer till the weeds dry
up, burned by frost,
and huge beacons
shine through
like planets submerged and rising.

Pioneer

Though it can live on water and air alone
the lichen is not ascetic,
goes where it can
find space.
Chalks off.
Flourishes on bark.
Is a family, not competitive.
Farms the rock itself and when it looks
like peeling paint and old maps
is most alive.
Munches the rock
and soils the bare clay
with its dead.
Until vegetation appears
and the luxuries of shade and decay.
Moves on to the open, the clean air.

Horace Pace

Just the other day I thought
of you for the first time
in years, cousin, and of the
cabin they built in the pines
on the west side of Uncle Jim's
hill, the shack of unpainted
undressed boards raised
for you to die in the last
winter before the war. Horace
you read and coughed there afternoons
with sun coming red through the
pines and your one window. All
the talk was Germany.
The preacher bibled by
to prod you toward salvation,
and couples your age courting
would fill the house
Sunday afternoons, your
father heard off
praying in the thicket. You
skeptic, witty, in love
with the draining weeks
of reality, the family's
last peaceful roman.
Dogs came to howl outside
and you could turn to
look through the trees upriver
toward the Chimneys and across the
bottoms to our graveyard
where in a few months you
and everything else would be
the same except the war.

Killing the Dog

Hoping he'll get run over, go off
on his own and die out of sight,
you put it off, can let no one else
do the amputation.
One of his eyes is a half

opened oyster, the other has the glaze
of infinity. He's deaf, no sense
of direction, control
of bowels or bladder. Goes everyday
shitting on doorsteps, stops traffic.

Strokes have burned off acres
of memory, bridges washed out. He's no
longer yours, but knows and backs
crippled when you come to kill.
Follow hating him for cheating

you of grace through snaky fields,
chiggers, through goldenrod, sweating
for a good shot, but he's gone.
Like when he ruined trout pools
you'd spent half an hour approaching

by diving in and thrashing downstream.
The running and anger make it easy. Find
him trembling, treed for
once by you and by age.
The shot heals but does not assuage.

Squirrel. Shadow

He stops at the lake
to lift a dry leaf off the water.
Minnows warm at the earth's hearth.
A butterfly shivers
its drop of art nouveau over the weeds
and a squirrel runs casting its tail on the sky.
The old man walks through fields
overturning rocks and boards
looking for an entrance.
Today the turning leaves remind
him of a rattlesnake, a briar licks his hand.
The sun focuses directly at his face
harvesting
itself and trailing off,
throws heavy gangplanks across the hill.

Clearing Newground

Loosened with mattocks and chopped
from rootholds, the last stumps are
left to be dragged to the pyre.
Tough cloth of topsoil unstrung,

roots pulled unnerving
and ungristling the ground.
Poplar roots wet and fat as worms
entangle twists of sweet sassafras.

The intricate feeders shaggy with hair
are gathered by the yard;
and the dirt, unlaced and

unpinned, is free to be worked in
specific tropes and turnings,
escape downhill in a few years.

Frozen Lake

Cobwebs and chicken tracks appear
on the surface near shore, thin
scum growing to
the iris of the lake.
Begins clotting and clouding
the deep pupil. Gets
hold of the body and
locks in place bank to bank.
The lake is paved with dry crust. Its
cap fits like a stovelid over
the busy currents where
trout circulate
alert as the juice in a battery.
Springs throb in the mud down there
and leaves settle in beds. A
muskrat ascends its duct.

Wind scars the warped rink.
Edges thaw by day and no longer
matching grind the banks. Laminations
of melt and snow.
The shores calibrate
with shelves as the lake
drops under its load.
Wind sands and draws
screws of snow off into the woods.

Sometime in March sun picks the icelock.
Heavy lids are
raised on each section and
rubble herds onto the
leeshore. In the shallows grass
leans free. Deep water stands.

Progeny

The ink cloud drifting
in the pond is
tiny catfish
swarming perpetually
out of shape shading
the mother.
She turns
and ties knots
in the shallows,
stirring the mess
of fry like
filings, stroking
in sweeps and
circles
until fed by their
movement through
the pond scum the
particles
eventually
precipitate. On
these hot days they
camouflage her watch like
floating
moss, each strand
an image of herself.

Polemic

A chunk of clay suddenly
breaks from the thawing
bank and rolling
over gravel is
embedded and
stamped with impressions
of weedstalks before
splashing into the
creek.
Lies in the clear
ripple like a brick
of pigment
dyeing a
plume downstream.
Smokes and dusts the
shoal-water,
its trail
widening to
cloud the whole
current where it slows
into a pool.
By noon the chunk
burns out,
scrubbed
small and fecal, hardly
noticeable among
the seed-bright rocks.

Flight of Mountains

Steep shoals
pyramid in the west,
high groves and
sacred
burial ranges
piled like thunderheads,
flap one on the
other to
high haze,
ladder up to the
dam holding back sky.
The great wings
back
each other
up all the way
to the final gap.
Clear weather
files the nick
sharp as
a gunsight.
I mean to climb
up there,
over the hogbacks and
heavy buttresses,
knowing hollows
and marshes
of meander
separate the
rough topologies, to
sit at the tip
of the breaking
looking over.

III.

Paradise's Fool

Climbing

Say the hillside pasture is the foot
of a long ramp running up to the first
tier of a ziggurat
and the ridge beyond steepens
up to another
shelf and the mountain
glides up to a table,
and nothing beyond that but
blue chimneys sharp against it.
Think how far that nothing goes and how wide.
Its other side touches the Other
Side. Though it's just three
big steps down to here
where plowed ground and cropped
grass are separate by a fence.

Rising a step at a time out of the valley—
finding stirrups in the dirt
to swing up on,
choosing
the next in mid-step
with no pause, one foot
rolling onto the next. Fingers
root for a hold in moss,
leaves, the dirt at your face.
And always the top just above with
the eastern sky pure,
almost black in the afternoon.
Once up rest
as in a bunk or hayloft
against the skyeave and look down.
Nothing to do but go down
and you go,
banking on rocks
and rappelling off saplings,
lose altitude so fast ears close,
dropping, parachuting,

till the ground holds out
on all sides,
thickets and marshes to crawl through.

At the timberline trees compact
and twist to hold in their sap against emptiness.
Forests give way to thickets that give
way to arctic moss and above just
weather busting rock on the pile.
From here the climb's rough
as the phrenology of mountains to look out on.
Lofty shore I climb out of the deep
spruce and rest on a ledge in the heather.
Foamy heather in the sun.
Tatterdemalion coastline. Nothing
ahead but clouds breaking spray on the turret
rocks. Let me camp here in the surf shrubs,
near the island's polar coign.

Sometimes I feel the seethe and crackle
of ions swept off the sun
as solar wind,
brushing the heat wool
and spiraling up blizzards
that far out cool and fall, each
particle refinding
its mate in the platinum mud.
As a tree sends out limbs grubbing
and the dirt's hungry for sun milk
through rot and leafmold,
mind too wants the slimy core
metals, whey and stink
of the smelter.
Wants the steel honey
of the blast furnace.
Eye climbs open and finds the sun
high over the river, the clear stuff
drifting all the way down to the sky sill.

Beans want to climb.
They lift themselves up
and feel around for something to hold to,
runners already kinked, constricting
on string or cornstalks, felted
to catch any surface.
But cucumbers prefer to spill
out of the ground and run down
hill holding leaves overhead.
Have the same inclination
as water,
to pour and keep going.
Aspire only to describe the terrain,
seek no skeleton.
So you train daily,
twisting the woolly runners on hemp.
Lifting and tying under armpits,
propping
so they stand
toward the azure they don't want.
And at the top fall over again, streaming
out kitetails, hunting the ground.

To live in the mountain high
as in an attic with
dormer windows
and balconies,
castellated ledges
looking out over the plain
inked green by the little
lost river hunting
a sandtrap to vanish in.
The cornfields and sheep
are descended to by
fitting hands and feet
like cogteeth in holes up and
down the cliff's sheer.
Cool in the rock,
wind this high

always freshing the recesses
and playing the tunneled
passages where
grain is heaped and
cisterns of water cool
under tribal paintings.
Images gathered like honey
and brought here. Cliffdwelling.

In the still
of early morning
smoke climbs
scandent
taking hold and
lifting high
on the coolness,
a few shifts
and twists
out of true
alignment but
raises like
a charmed snake
from the house
clinging
acrobatically
to altitude,
and jacking almost
straight plumbs
the upper air
still reaching,
touches
a current
that spreads it
over the valley.

The two big pines that planted the grove
below stood among hardwoods.
Their shade was a dank
yard, briary

tent, drifted with tufts
of needles from the heights.
The voices in the towers became
an obsession.
Looking up one of the masts
radiating its spokes you
saw no further
than the first branches.
Limbs near the ground had fallen
but the stubs remained in the bark
or cores of the stubs pegging
the battlement-sized base.
Climb up them to the first limbs (a pop
warning how much weight to trust).
From there on it's mounting
a spiral ladder, brushing
aside to find the next hold.
A dry limb breaks
numbing the hands, sickens
bones. The trunk becomes
tree-sized, green leathery bark.
A squirrel's nest stuffed in the forks.
Resined hands grip anything.
Already above the hardwoods, looking
out windows in the branches.
Swaying now up into
the christmastree top
and easing into a saddle of limbs
just under the tip. Body weight
makes the sway longer, like a metronome,
going far out over the other trees
and back, canter holding
the bristly reins
looking over the pines
to the pasture. The steed takes off
as wind returns
spilling its voice
around and below you.

Rice

The most fertile grain would be
amphibious, roots in dirt, stalks in water,
and leaves wicking the sun.
The charge of three dominions
rushes through the filaments hotter
by friction and interreference than a spree

of acids. Sugars coil in solution.
Mud bristles like a mind submerged
out of ego into reverie but full
sized and available
just under the loosening film and urged
by heat to sweat out an explosion

of seed, spraying pure carats. As if
land sunk and water risen flush with land
achieve critical mass.
Register the sun's vast
pressure by darkening leaves and
stretching stalks with the lift

of hydraulic cylinders. The short tined
feet heave in the sty of hotbeds
terraced around the hill like threads
of a screw rearing stychomythic
crops afloat, quick
as if hoisted in locks of time.

Compass

One direction, one line of reference,
is all you need to start from
to go anywhere.
And though we don't
the blue sliver
hears
and responds,
aligning with its desire,
to a wind more subtle
than motion. Nervous,
alert,
always remembering
to point home,
a clock with one instant.
Though unsteady as mercury
and constant
only in approximation,
it lays off the horizon, protracting
the possible.

Volunteer

Praise what survives
its season of domestication
and sprouts along the margin,
among next year's crop.

Aggressive species ignore
the fences and boundary lines
of rotation to emigrate.

Praise blooded varieties returning
to the wild.

Spontaneous replanting be praised. Let
self-sowers reverdure the earth.

Let every garden and tiergarten and
sunken eden leak
breeds that multiply
to the limits of resource.

Praise all escapes
and trailing shrubs, runners that
spill out of culture
and reseed themselves.

Let volunteers find accommodation.

Witch Hazel

After the failure of vegetation,
the leaves' ripening and fall of
seed, while the summer's
mail is whirled

against the moon like geese
and loaded high in thickets,
when the orchards are stripped
and cornfields stink

scatologically, find
along the forest margins
and creek banks this
small shrub that held back in

flowering time, hoarded its
best sap through the sixth-month
plenty and dog days, and
harvest luau,

waiting for the first cool
afternoons to
open its heat to the
older sun, visible

now to all bees for
orgies,
dipping black wands to
find honey, corrupting the

grammar of the seasons for
a mardi gras above the dank
and souring competition,
flicking seeds on snow.

Fall

Now rain strafes the morning hills
and trees spend their lucre
onto the sky—
the sewers of the field are opened.
When the storm hits into the maples
it would seem that great
tokamak the sun is molting for
the woods are light incarnate.
Yes I too, looking at the rubble,
believe we have passed
a hundred times through
the guts of earthworms and
bless those transformations.
Coming in I bring
a seasoned log to your fireplace.

Tell

Coming on a hill many stories
above the grasslands
and wastes of far-reaching canals.
Rain and high wind have exposed
bits of pottery and brick
around the summit.
A wall corner shows. Digging,
fortresses filled with blowing
dirt raise battlements
built on the ruins of others
ancient to them.
And those walls rest
like successive stages of
etymology on foundations and
castellations of temple-brothels
over cellar libraries.
Peeling off a few more centuries finds
a mausoleum unsealed and robbed
before the body melted.
Shoveling through silt, lamina
of urns, weapons, after
a few thousand years to arrive
beyond assembling and restoration
at virgin soil, without clue,
no origin. There at the center
of the first hill just
sandstorms leveling and filling
all depressions, building ramps
up and over walls, and below that
nothing but mud where once
some river anointing
the steppes turned back to the sea,
and dust saying anathema.

Copse

What a crowding at the boundary
between field and wood, a thrusting
out between the shade and cultivated ground.
Shielded by trees from wind
and frost, yet open to the sun,
the margin fills with seedlings and every

gap between seedlings with weeds. Thin
sprays of ironweed, thistle lofts
and turrets. Fountains of sweetshrub
confront and oppose, and broomsedge silkens
up to the fence and beyond, flows
swirling through alcoves into the pines.

Here at its shoreline the field
trails eddies of rye clockwising off
into brush. There is a rush to fill
every matchbox of space. This is the roost
of fugitives, a stateline perfect
for getaways either direction, concealed.

Mice traffic from field to stash, give
moles their preference of laidby soil
under pokeweeds. Frontiers of rockpiles
and rotting stumps nest rattlers.
Because it cannot survive
mowing ironweed thrives

here. And lanterned sumac reaches from behind
the first ranks putting out a sign.
Every bush and sapling jams
its limbs to the frontage, crams hoping
to get a view, plugs every chink
to the open along the fireline

where wild spills through like magma shot
from below and strewing ragweed into the rows.

Briars splash and throw out barricades,
cast fishing with tufts of hair over rabbit
trails, grapple. Cobs left by squirrels
blacken on the shelf where the plowing stops.

Oblique

Take earth, the astigmatic
earth, its biases
and shifty poles.

Take askewness, the wobbles
and cycles that though
imperfect
engender and evolve through
orbits that resolve into orbits.

The slant
moderates and tempers,
gives privilege by turns,
extending summer
beyond Capricorn and Cancer,
strums the equatorial
belt, fattening the tropics.

Flatboat

I could go along with this:
making a page out of the woods wherever
we come out fronting the river.
Just throw together
a raft with walls, a tray
of timber that's available to carry
us out on the current with maybe
a hut in one corner,
its floor just above water,
and a long-poled sweep made from
a wagonseat steering in the rear
around sandbars and keeping clear
of the big steamers' wash.
Just drifting, that's me, lost
and singing in the river night past
towns and ferrylandings, going by
unlighted farms—just the
swish of sweep and crickets in
the meadows, and a lantern on
the pole to punch the rising mist.
And when the wide seedbox
of cattle and hogs and implements
gets all floated down that open
highway in the wilderness, why, tie up and sell
it by the cord, or dismantle
and burn, or just abandon.
I like to make things that can
be left like water where their use ends,
that saddle a river's back
and take us part-way cross continent.

Privilege

The overly advantaged
remind me of the young birch
that planted by a seed floating
to rest on a stump
takes root in the damp

composting rings and sprouts
prodigious, drinking
even in dry weather from
its spongy mesa. Lifted free
of floor growth, above competing moss

and poison ivy, it gets a headstart
from the decaying reservoir
that puts it up among the older
trees in a decade and sends
long feeders and a tap

down through the capillaries of
spunk and rotten sheathing into
the base of its host.
The problem manifests when
the privileging pedestal

erodes from its grasp
and the young birch,
stranded three feet out of dirt
must trust its full weight to
slender roots exposed above soil.

Beached

Their inner ears and sonar guidance
systems eaten by worms
whales sometimes run aground
or stun themselves colliding
on maneuvers.

Washed up and stranded
by low tide they pant and blow
among the breakers, crushed
out of water by their
own weight, bellies

cut by sand. Their
arctic insulation's so efficient
they broil from
body heat out of
refrigerating depth,

skin blistered by sunburn
and exposure.
In a few hours they
lie delirious with pneumonia,
great cocks extended in mud.

The outer flesh already stinks.
The mountains
swell in
mockery of tumescence
and often explode

flinging tons of offal down
the beach. Some lie
days in massy fever, unable to hear
the others sing
in the deep canyons, flit

and call from the hollows and steep
meadows, chirping
through forests of light, in
touch with all other herds
within maybe a thousand miles.

Buffalos in Blizzard

When a big one hits out there
on the plains of North Dakota they
stop and stand, let
their enemy the wind
do the marching,
let the thick moldy air get
lost and go in circles
dragging the drifts and coulees.
Old buffalo he won't
even try for a ditch or
rock to hide in the shade of,
just stands there in the mounting
snow like stonehenge chewing
hot cud belched
up from his stomachs
and smoldering steam
while his wool cakes with
sediments.
And sinks down to sleep in the warm
hill of himself while wind
deflected hunts
in canyons and silos overhead.

Ice Worm

That habits the puddled feoffments
on glaciers unlikely
as a forest fire in Antarctica or green
meadows on the moon. That segments

life in the transparent jeweled soil
pushing out each morning to feed in a pool
of melt on manna of pollen
and algae wind lays there. That
grazes and lazes in the sun-expanded lens

and living high in the white aeolian zone
fed by air itself at the focal point
of its crystal dish observes the agon
of hot star on the sugarfields and lakes joining

the sky. And leaves before dark freezes
the puddle reentering through its pore the
insulating dungeons
while the million-ply gloamy sleep
of ice keeps taking up its bed on the ozone
ledges and going down to sea.

Midnight Sun

To my northern humor release
comes late and goes early,
but comes when it does with such
strength everything catapults
into growth out of

taiga and muskeg. The air
fills with thirsty frenzy and glaring
packice breaks shelving
back onto itself toward the pole.
Revenant fowl

clutter tundra and shore.
The grass untelescoping bores
in roots as the permafrost sinks
out of reach. Whales crowd inky
inlets and gravel washed out

of the mountains to the south
gems the auriferous mud
when ice breaks its showcase.
Dirt heaves in labor.
The sun never sets on this brief empire

of creation compressed so small
every molecule's candescent and all
seasons rub hot like brushes
of a generator dusting and cutting
lines of force. Where

the magnetic fountains rears
I crowd my exhilarations
into a camera flash. Shunned
by the long deliberate year
I make these few midnights solar

and strike into the long night of need
a rank garden, an eden.

Paradise's Fool

In the appletree abloom at the field's
edge and in the hummingbird's
nest of moss and plantdown,

in the canticles of the star maiden
and subtle
aesthetics of failure,

the severalty of tidelands, duff
of fencerows, word amulets, stench of traffic
in the electron, I

am paradise's fool.
See the grapery and mariculture, whole
alloys of people, singing plants,

nut groves and
the clitoris sharp as a phonograph needle
scoring circles of music.

Lo, worlds without beginning in
the spring's contact lens,
the haunted well and camphorwood.

Neither in surview nor sweet veld
do I escape the terror,
the presence of the comforter.

TRUNK & THICKET

For William Harmon

PART I

TRUNK & THICKET

Think of looking in the trunk, of going
up to the attic in late summer
where wasps crust
the windows and spit past so
close they lift a strand of hair
and the guts of a piano
are spilled among fruit jars and stacks
of newspapers. Dry heat near
the chimney is empty of oxygen.
The trunk as if inflated
bulges, a compact
coffin. The rustmolten lock
pulls out by the screws, leather
dry as hair, brass knobs on the corners
scabbed blue. The lid raises warped

on trays of recent leavings. Then a wadded
funeral flag they handed my grandpa
at the service for my uncle after
the war, floating on the junk beneath,
and the understrata bear
report cards, rationbooks and arrowheads,
birth certificates and snapshots of
a baptizing, older and better arranged than
the stuff on top. Packed in the depths,
a blanket, armistice headlines, shoetree,
scab of tacks rusted together. All pressed and
composting, fuse with paper in a drymelt.
This archaeology of going up to the attic
to dig and dig up whatever connects, throws
open a door out of the present, for there
is nothing here but the clock-wise turning
stone of ambition on the right and
the counterclock-wise turning stone
of failure on the left, closing to grind.

Hoping something can be learned
if I read memory fine enough,
will find encoded like some gene
or microfilm the key to my survival
in the ordinary incident or image that
washes up.

I want to go out with a flashlight in
the bright noon and shine a spot on the clutter,
find heating up at the focal point, in the
matted grass and random piles of
scantling, something buried for decades
that suddenly flares and lights up
a corner long forgotten. Once I
planted a walnut in the fall, promising
to dig it up on Christmas, but forgot,
years later noticing a tree on the spot.

                    *

Earliest memory:
being carried home on my
father's shoulder and waking
to see the stars aswing as though
on strings, or the same in daytime
and looking down at green chewing gum
wrappers in the parkinglot sand.
Or standing by the log barn
at cold milking time. In the Blue
Ridge everyone felt inferior:

mountain folk to valley, valley to
village, village to town. All
felt beneath lowcountry southerns
swarming in from Charleston, Miami,
the legacy of long isolation, poverty.
I was given a quarter once to walk

barefoot on road gravel for the kids
to see and did. The shame of driving
through town in a pickup is matched
by nothing but the shame of having no

truck at all. Blame the shouter with
spit on his chin, the blue
mountains themselves, and the brooding
hideaway types who settled there.
The rest crossed over west
after the war. Though mountain people
owned no slaves and little else, and were
culturally discrete from the rest
of the South, they got drafted too.
Many deserted north or hid out
in caves, making liquor same
as before; one of my distant
cousins spent three years at home
in the attic until an informer
brought the guard. While they searched
downstairs he jumped from the gable
window and broke a kneecap, but
kept running, was shot in
the back climbing the snake
fence into the orchard.

                        *

After a rain in May
the mountains look like
salad churned fresh
and far. It's true
the Blue Ridge was made
by turbulent matter
thrust up from deep in
the mantle and then pinched
off underneath as the

opposing plates ran
together. No other mountains
have the same beaten
shapes. No fault lines
or long running troughs
as in the Poconos or
Alleghenies. They're a kind
of island floating on the
continent. Some of the peaks
are called Islands of Canada,
the summits being misty
groves of fir and spruce
native to Ontario. The ground
up there is peatmoss a foot
deep, each fallen log a dugout
growing seedlings.
Between lightning and logging
and aphids the greencapped
peaks are now mostly scalds
and blasted meadows. Clouds
drifting over Georgia and
the Piedmont hit the cool
updrafts there and collapse.

And always the desire is for the wind
behind the first wind, that comes
after and beyond the initial
inspiration, that comes pushing
and bearing up, propelling no matter
what halts and turns, the perpetual
deep roar taking over after the first
few strokes. The marriage, the recognition
of the transformation behind the transformations.
The voice-river keeps coming into
view around the bend of the second.
According to my mother I was born
tongue-tied; the tip was knitted to

the base of my mouth by a thread
of tissue. Six weeks after birth they
snipped it free. Sometimes it still
feels sewn down. Turning suddenly I
can't speak; a word swells in my throat
and chokes. My tongue wallows, stuck
helpless in mud. The skin tightens on
my forehead, face in hell. Strangling
I disguise a retreat. Never trust words
to bear up; skate quick over the thin
skim of sentences, or slow down almost to
a pause and build a syllable at a time
on the footing of silence.

Like lakedwellers we live far out from
shore on thin pilings of language nailed
down into mud, fish and toilet from the
doors of our fragile towers, ropes
pulled up, never hearing the currents
nudge against the stilts or
fog maul through the scaffolding except
maybe late in sleep.

*

High up on its mansard
the mountain after a
wetspell calves; a haunch
of rainmushy ridge
sags tearing root
connections and pulls
a sheet of topsoil off the
rockface greased with clay.
The boulder exposed tilts
in fat mud, rolls out of
its socket and lurching
newborn through slidedirt

accelerates crashing on trees
and other rocks, is altered
before coming to rest.
Lies full in the level woods
as a larva, negative cave
pushed out and dominating
the spill. On the altar
lichen and thaw burn slowly,
weather eats a slow meal.
After a summer day flies
light to its warmth and cling,
drop off with the draining
calories. My uncles used to
go to a house-sized boulder
in the woods in time of trouble.
It rose through the pines and
above leaning out a shelter
blackened by campfires.
Leaned out so far you'd
expect to see it fall, like
a wave breaking. Called
the prayer rock. No vines
scaled its ramparts, no
other boulders or fragments
around. Only the distant
cliff from which it broke
and rolled. Each rock is a
wornout statue, a monument
chipped from history and
subliming in time, features
dulled like a snowman's.
Marks a specific era until
its molecules are dispersed
by wear, spit out in wind
and spilled downhill like
seeds. Whether aligned in walls
that topple over and lie

random in the fields, or
polished like beans in the
dry creek trough of summer,
a few painted with silt, but
most shiny, all corners and
teeth worn, pouring like buttons
downhill and sliding easy as
bearings under the stream,
lotioning and jeweling its
movement, shrinking under the
traffic. Another memory,
Buzzard Rock up there,
grayface in waning summer, coming
out full in winter. Aunt Idy
said it would break off and roll
down one day, had a crack you
couldn't fit a knife in when
she was a girl, now three
feet wide. High as thunder.

*

Even in deepest space the voice
is sphygmic, hidden beat
of pulsars. Placing a big
stethoscope to night
the chants are deafening,
like a geigercounter going mad
when its nerve end is touched
to the uranium filling in a rock.

*

Nobody in my family ever went off on public works for more than
a few weeks, always quit or fired. One uncle attended barber school
and cut hair at the army base in Columbia during the war. Back
home by Christmas he said, "Can't cut a head of hair to please them

Yankee officers, smart-talking sons of bitches." At the same time
my father went off to paint barracks at Camp Croft, and the next
year at Fort Bragg, and quit both, and finally Cherry Point Marine
Base on the coast, and quit. Rawhiding foreman, bash him over the
head with a shovel if he talks too rough. I ain't spending my life
smothering in no cottonmill.

*

Never could look in a crock
of milk going blinky,
the oily gobs separating
and marbling in the vomit-rich sour,
without thinking of great-grandpa
sitting there on the porch
driving the plunger like a piston
to agitate the sweet nuggets
to the surface to be skimmed off and pressed
empty of whey; he's looking down the
valley toward Meetinghouse Mountain
when all fades out. He falls
knocking the churn over and
spilling clabber onto the yard
where the chickens rush to start pecking.
Not a month before that his son
sat on the bars of the gap
waiting for him to return from
mill, saw him coming up the hollow
in a suit of clothes.
When he was close enough to speak
the son turned to greet him but
found no one in sight in all the valley.

*

It is said the Pueblo elders in the kiva, their half-sunken meeting
room, keep a hole in the center symbolic of the place where their

ancestors emerged. Around the well they gather both to honor
and to guard the entrance to this realm. There in the darkroom
where new images appear they're dangerously close to the eruption.
Sometimes I feel that near the springhead when a phrase comes
right with no act of my own and reveals something just beyond my
apprehension, as if I had brushed close to the whitehot with only the
faintest recognition. As if I lived mostly within the walls of dead air
space where waves severely dampened by one panel are erased by
the second. Think of the sounds absorbed and buried between, as
in the space between one skull and another or that second skull the
sky, for which these words would be writs of habeas corpus. Speak
for the inarticulate, the neurotically shy, for the silent son who sits
by the stove in the mountain kitchen.

*

Used to go down to Ulyss Bane's
garage by the highway, housed
in a big tin shed built
with money paid
when his third son was
hit by a car. Had his carhospital
there on the dirt floor, tables
piled with dirty tools
and a vise worked loose
on its bolts unsteady even
while its jaws held tight.
Grease slugs curled in the dust.
He worked by a single
troublelight while
junk lurked to the ceiling
in corners like exotic weeds
and molds. A sooty lushness of
metal. Hands cut and mashed
on obstinate parts for
fifty years.
Got started with a

fifteen dollar Model T
and a correspondence course
from Chicago taken jointly with
his brother to save money. His
oldest son they found sunk
with his girl in a car in a South
Carolina lake. Ulyss
had a vision that if he went
to a tree by the fruitstand
down the highway
on a certain night something
would be revealed to him,
but didn't go for fear the news
would be worse than ignorance.
The car on its axles with cat
tracks over the hood and glass
was the deathcar Junior
and his brother went to sleep
in one Christmas Eve with
the motor running. Its
trunk is the only thing on the place
that locks so he stores the best
tools and new parts there
and uses it also for cash.

*

My mother used
the calendar as eyechart, the yellowing newsprint page
of the month exposed. Sundays looked contiguous but
I learned they dragged the simple days like tails.
And on the chart of coming days and those
already passed, pencilings and circles, notes
scribbled about cows bred and hens set, when someone
was due to leave for the army. The cobbling
through which the present had run
filling each separate lock and flowing

on with no pause. A new calendar arrives in
the mail before Christmas and is hung
behind the old until
time for transfer, an effortless
shift from one reel to another.
The days caught in the net there,
aligned neat as the lattice of a crystal,
grow without stopping on
the solution of human consciousness.

*

A red spider fattens into the hill, feeding
through legs extended in
topsoil and delicate root circuitry.
Burns the hill, yet is a part of the hill
much as the grass it replaces or
boulders that float up.
Even the junk collecting around
the windfall at the gully's mouth
becomes part of the hill's shape automatically.
The rough pile fits with clay shoals and
gutting spill of runoff after a summer
shower. Swarming vines embellishing
the brush are as much a part of the hill's
features as gravity. The wash exposes
a rockvein breaking into quartz teeth.

*

When my father used to walk his trapline he could remember
passing a particular tree or bend in the trail what he was thinking
when he came that way before. Same trail, same tree, but a different
state of mind. The trapline is thrown out over the watersheds
and the trapper must wade out to visit each set. He can be a
sharpshooter using a few delicate sets for mink or shotgun with a
trap below every muskrat slide. Daily navigating the high peaks and

secluded meadows and valleys, the trail invisible to a passerby. The
traps and deadfalls wait all night, triggers sensitive as eardrums,
extensions of the senses. The dirt snaps like a shark and won't let
go. Mink or rat set deep enough to drown. A fox will circle on the
chain grinning with pain, the bobcat crouches hissing. A marten
streams black under ice, unreachable till thaw. Peeled like fruit the
critter's hairy sock is harvest. Nailed scab-like to the crib they cure
in late winter, a bulletin board of pubic scalps.

*

Down at the sandbar, what a place
to hang around in summer. Little
beach in the woods where minnows
sow the shallows and bubbles heat
focal points on the bottom. Bits
of glass and metallic trash stud
the tongue of accretion. The
outermost isthmus even in drought
is damp a few inches down. The
creek unsnarling from its crook
acts as a reflector doubly lighting
the strand bleached white as meal.
Now a sandpump is raised on the
bank and a black hose sneaks down
into the pool to draw off the floor.
Sticks and leaves rush to the
strainerhead drinking gritty slush
swallowed up and sprayed out on
the screen, yards of wet creek floor
splashing into the bins.
The diesel roars day and night,
its eye penetrating to the very
foundations of the stream and counting
into its hourglass coffers, safe from
the current, the valley's loose teeth.

But the real word I guess, the
motif, is home. Homecoming. Homing.
How to touch base.
In the meantime, ultimately,
home may be whatever pulls
and keeps in motion. The phrase
only half understood when spoken
hardens into focus out there at a distance.
Just the ongoing motion of the voice
unlatches things in the mind
like spring rain soaking in, frees
the almost-perceived into music that
goes enjamming,
turning through rocks and trash.

Homing is the act of stopping where
you are and waiting for the stars
to come out, nightvision.
By describing the terrain
or a weather instrument's scrawl
we locate the median, the watertable
just below.
These swings away lead us back
homing on the quiddity.
Coming down the homestretch
with the heightened sense of always
arriving in the present.

*

Let the stubbled fields and anthologies
confer in camera,
whirring the brushes of
the generator. Place suffering
and grief in a cybernetic equation
with sufficient reason, plenitude.
Syndics, hospice, oratorios,

the dumps behind groceries,
refuse and offal of slaughterhouse,
trunks of charnel, embalmed codes
of decorum, the midden and compost, shames
of poverty. Fire the limestone
of institutions, smelt humanism for
recycling. Transduce the
chemical scums on ponds, slime of imagination,
aluminum mud. I want to come home to the present, to
the wreckage thrown up as futures.

*

After the deposit of seed, after
the salting and sidedressing, thinning
and replanting gaps, heaping over
new roots with cultivator and sweep, after
the cut weedstubs bleed wet spots
in the dirt, and cut leaves crumble like
flakes of dried blood in the sun,
comes the laying by.
The loam crusts
and is tamped by rain.
Needles and sawbriars are back
in a week. Vines cast out
blooms over the surface and the ranks
of corn dissolve in proliferation
and diversity. Smut swarms
to cornjoints and on the shaded
ground clods soften in the rain
and solder to the scab.

*

Think of winter wheat out there, the
lush mat of it pressed down by two feet
of snow, while the juice-filled blades feed

on the solar sediments in the crystals,
breathe the snow's trapped atmospheres and
charge the snow with nitrogen.
Stems fatten insulated by ice
from scorching wind while
blizzards pluck and clean the
glazed fields and drifts climb into
the hedgerows. Leaves nibbling down there
like minnows, each blade cutting
a sheath to grow in.

*

Like the filament of a darkroom
lamp the vine grows
in the gloom of Wall Holler,
lit by mold and touched only by
moths and wailing mosquitoes;
until a cow, lost in the brush of the
ravine, comes to the bank above the spring
and crops the tender stem,
then spurred by flies
wanders back out
and reaches the gap by
milking time, udder scratched
and whelked. The weed venom
enters the milk intact
and strikes the drinker after midnight,
attacking nerves and
imitating flu until too
late. By morning he's gutted
by fever, tongue swollen like a black
mushroom out of his throat. Milksick.

My mother had a friend who off
and on lost her voice.
One year at Christmas she'd talk normally;
the next summer we'd meet her on the street
during Apple Festival and be
greeted by a coarse whisper that
sometimes rose to a hiss but
seemed not to come from her, or at least
not from her mouth.
As if she were haunted and
a demon croaked inside her. I
avoided her kiss and kind smiling eyes.
The affliction, nervous, came on without
warning and would leave suddenly.
Neither hypnosis nor drugs would help.
She said once it felt as if
her larynx froze in paralysis.
The harder she tried the less came through,
syllables melting and tearing like paper.
She must wait and whisper, straining
to forget the voice out of hiding.

*

Splitting rails is important
in our history as splitting atoms.
I came on the remains of a snake fence
in the woods the other day, tacking out through trees,
its bars mostly spilled and soaking into the leaves
since the last century.

A few corners still interlock, still
neatly tied and plumb. Built
back when margins were generous, the bracing
sleepers could be taken down and reset without tools.
Must have been comforting to see those fences
whip out along the edge of clearings

and chinked tight with snow serve as windbreak
for stock no barbed wire could shield,
cranking out lightning
over the hills, stitching
homesteads and settlements together.

Looked makeshift, washed up at high
floodmark, rough chain spun from trees.
Pinked borders and sawed thickets down to size,
wavelength and amplitude accommodating
boulders, stumps. Stopped dead
at the stream's edge.

*

Walking the drained beach you
find anything washed up,
spurs and anchors of wood scrubbed
down to corefibers, polished
jewelhard knots where the tree
suffered galls. Brittle oak
endures longest, peeled and salted
in the vats of ocean, bled sapless
and embalmed in the currents far
off shore and thrown back to land
again shrunk to scar tissue lasting
lifetimes beyond the healthy wood.
What proofs do we have of continuity?
The mind goes out mowing with its
caliper. What is its critical mass?
Hard to see the great curve for
ditches and brush, the forward
motion only faintly discernible
among detours, endless backtrackings.
But even while stopped I know it's
completing itself apart from me,
the way like a stranger I keep
running into.

*

In these hills the
moon like a druid in
wrinkled silk steps
out of the pines and
roves on the night
spelling with the
astronoming eye, hurries
through cliffrock,
peaks of thrown spray.
Catches on a scrap of
deep space. Tall grass
and weeds wade in the
water, oaks on the hill
point to the deep center,
advance separately over
the rocking terrain,
but get no closer, can't
leave the quick meadow
inside the pond.

*

Truck. The word has troubling
associations. In the first grade
we read about boys and girls who
gathered truck on their street
to be carried to the city dump.
None of us lived on a street or
had fathers who drove off to work
in the morning dressed in Sunday
clothes. We called it trash. Until
I was nine we had no truck and
went to town with Uncle in his old
army rig. Always had to ask, beg,
pay him to take us, though he was
going already every Friday to the
checkered feedstore on south Main,
and taking eggs to the grocery.

Had to sit squeezed in, legs
carefully arranged around baskets
of eggs. Always a fuss. Sometimes
a crate of squawking chickens in
the back. Once when it rained and
he forgot the tarpaulin we rode
with peeping chicks and a bag of
shorts, Uncle hollering all the
way, threatening to run the truck
off the road. Junior:

"We had two trucks at the electric plant for carrying trash. Before
my promotion I drove one and my cousin the other. We made three
runs a day, sometimes when they were running the big transformers
which had wooden crates instead of cardboard four or five. It
was dirty work at first, especially the loading. They bring it to the
dock in bins and with a little footwork you can dump it in without
touching anything, including the oily stuff and paper from the paint
booths. First week on the job I wore old jeans and army boots, but
after that I bought good clothes. Where you're around dirt people
expect you to be dirty and it looks especially good if you're neat
and surprise them. So with the first checks I started going over to
the men's stores in Asheville for ten and twelve dollar shirts and
good Bostonian shoes. Mostly I never got them dirty on the job I
was so careful. We had a kind of contest to see who could dress
best without getting dirty. Once I touched something splashed by
that acid machine and burnt two holes in twenty-dollar pants. After
that I watched out. I kept the cab clean too by keeping my shoes
clean, which was pretty hard at the dump where it was dusty in
summer. We filled up the long gully in Hensley's pasture all the way
to the branch. The water running out of there began to look kind
of orange from coming through that paint-soaked paper and wood.
Now they bulldozed it over."

*

When my father stretched the deerhide on the barn
and tacked the corners and inlets like a
flattened tent, bits of meat
still colored the shiny skin. He
scraped it smooth as a diploma and let

it yellow, a leaf pinned to the boards. Next
year it still spread there, wings browning and
stiffening to a crust set with dauber panpipes. And
tearing like a scab

from the nail-teeth and flapping its
rags eaten by rats.

*

See the powerful enjambment
of a stream carried on and over
its rocks, sometimes pausing
in deep pools and then darting
in a channel or spread thin
over rockface, but always
careering, always arriving
and leaving at once, always on
its way. At the top of the ridge
water searches meticulously
through gravel and weeds for
a way out, goes shining its
flashlight and feeling around,
backtracks and hesitates swelling,
then bypasses the obstacle, always
finding an exit. Rainwater
rallies, shouts in the ditch for
hours. Weeds by the rush are
undercut. Drills potholes and
ties off boulders, strips down
to clay and cobbles a bed for

itself. The precedent, the first
twitch, becomes habit and
hardened by use aims
instinctively, usage becoming
tradition, institution,
incontrovertibly the way.

*

                    Follow
backcountry trails and old
haulroads. Both
canals and big highways refuse to
describe the terrain, ignore all
but the most long-held rise and fall,
their wavelength stretched out
by fill and bridges.
The canal steers water
above valleys and out through
woods and low gaps, passes
through swamps defended by walls, secure
from stagnation by motion. Assembles
feeder creeks and taps in and out
of lakes, sometimes filling a lock,
always passing the burden on.

Cannot gather or dissipate, cannot
give way to gravity and spill
out before arriving. So the
superhighway runs out on its
levee over cornfields and cuts
diagonally between hills. Is
elevated not to negotiate the gnarled
runs and stumble over logs. Shoots
high over portages, fords, briarpatches,
thrusts through a gutted hill dropping
by millions of years of strata

every second. Does not have to prove
each crumpling ditch.
But the portages
and interruptions count. The
failure to get through
gives the chance to climb,
hauling canoe and equipment over
the steep ledge and under hemlocks
to a point surveying the rivershed.

*

Think of those princes of the church militant
who penetrated to the heart of the continent
while the English were struggling on the Atlantic
seaboard. Canoeing up the Ottawa and chain of lakes
from the St. Lawrence they reached by a short portage
the waters of the interior opening a passage
to the great west, and by another short carry
the Mississippi. Someone said the other day the
spot where they buried Marquette at thirty-seven
on the straits of Mackinaw has a rusted marker grown
over with weeds. But mostly think of La Salle, that
haughty visionary who first conceived the secular
empire of the west, and maddened by the tricks
of conniving Jesuits and treason among his
followers wandered lost in the marshes
of the Texas coast until surviving snakes and
fever and hostile natives he was murdered by his men.
His daydreams were two hundred years
out of phase with realization. Remember him.

*

It's easy in the Blue Ridge to imagine
you're out surfing on swells slowed
in time to imperceptible rocking.

I have sat on the south slopes on warm winter
afternoons just under the crest, out of reach of
wind compressing over the rim, and imagined deep under
me the trough where lighted fish dart and hover,
transparent eels swirling shock in vats of
pressure. Whales down there sing like birds
in the floor currents, call from the seamounts
and buried meadows. Grazing north they mote the
gulfstream bawling, erupt and blow, swoop out
of sound and return chirping through forests of
light, gilling out the rich impurities.

*

Out where a clearing's almost
grown over, the appletree
holds out, near the cellar
and old junipers. The fruit
comes smaller each year but
loads the black limbs into the
weeds. After frost the grass
is filled, rolling under the
feet and crushing, jassackets
busy in the cracked ones.
The whole area is redolent.
Some roll down against a log
and accumulate a rich pool.
Each has at least one good
side, a bite at the peak of
ripeness. I try as many as I
can, each tasting slightly
different.

*

To think matter itself is an
abyss. We can fall into the

distances of a boulder, right
through the crumpled surface
and behind the crushed-together
grains, flecks of mineral swelling
and separating into floes, past
the nuclear vapors toward flicking
insects of the core, past
blazing planets locked in orbit
of the prickling dark. But what
arrangements we find of the nothing,
here on the highwire of the senses.
Walking above the gulf, funambulists
extraordinaire. And the cool rockface
smokes and stinks as we hammer it
into shape.

*

Stars shiver up and break surface,
each a different color and size,
come on like crickets at random taking
posts and holding them, these points
of reference on which time is read
and we navigate and fix coordinates,
mythologies, foretell. The mind out
there a cloud chamber where motions
strike trails and storms of luminous dust.
Choose a gap in the sky and watch
it fill and the blanks between
the new stars fill, the planets
now flaring like suns in the foreground
blinding while you look deeper at the
outposts and frontiers; beacons appear
and still more behind them and still
beyond others light cities and
mountain ranges. Nearby at the lighted
window moths revolve like moons.
Inside the table is set for supper.

I've found my imaginings like sanghunting, something almost impossible to reproduce domestically once brought in from the wild. Half my family at one time or another in the old days went after ginseng. Before there was any industry at all in the mountains short of hewing crossties from dead chestnuts, they gathered the herb on wooded slopes just at the jumpoff into South Carolina and in a few sheltered hollows. Good dry roots brought thirty dollars a pound, but it might take two months to find them. Scattered unpredictably, few grew in one place. For decades they ranged pretending to hunt squirrels or be fishing and beeing, finding a plant or two hidden in underbrush, every year going out further and finding less. I've found most other things similar. After discovering a few at my feet and those in the foreground and nearby woods I have to go out far and wait long in all weather to get at the roots. Always making for the off-the-trail headwaters, the margins between watersheds, among the tangles of wild grape strangling a cucumber tree and deep in the ambiguous flatwoods where nothing seems to flow any direction. And found the succulent will not transplant, will be stolen and sold to China, will take a lifetime to mature. That crop is like topsoil getting thinner and thinner. Still I mean to move on, get up early and put some biscuits and meat in my pocket, be far back by sunup.

PART II

HOMECOMING

Our church held homecoming every year the third Sunday in August. The excuse for the annual picnic was it gave former members who had moved away and relatives and friends from nearby communities a chance to come back and visit. Besides the Christmas program it was the only time in the year for the congregation to enjoy its gathering free from the tensions of preaching and saving.

My great-great-grandfather had given land for the church at almost the exact center of the community of Green River. First, they met in a log building that doubled as a schoolhouse for two or three months in winter. It stood at the foot of a steep ridge that came to be called Meetinghouse Mountain. In the decade after the Civil War a white frame church was built and the grounds landscaped.

On the Saturday afternoon before homecoming the men and boys would gather to set up the tables. We carried planks and sawhorses from the basement of the church down to the shade under the great oaks along one edge of the parking lot. Those five trees had been on the property when it was deeded, and were a remnant of the virgin forest that once covered the mountains. They compared in size with the stands of tulip poplar and hemlock in the Joyce Kilmer Memorial Forest near Robbinsville, where a good tract of the original timber was salvaged from the logging companies and preserved. They seemed to spread almost as wide as their ninety or hundred-foot height, trunks thick and rough as ancient masonry. One had an enormous gall at its base which had hollowed out into a cave big enough for a small child to play in. On summer afternoons wind always seemed to be sliding up the valley from the river, cooling their shade.

While we lugged the boards and kegs of nails, those handy at carpentry would be assembling the table. It was interesting that many of the back-sliders, including my uncle who never came to church otherwise and drank heavily, came every year to help set up the long picnic table. Always cheerful, the taint of corn on his breath, he worked side by side with the deacons. The talk was easy, never religious. He would even discuss drinking and making liquor, but as though it was something he did in the past and quit long ago. "You know I never hurt nobody but when I was sober. When I cut that Howard boy down at Chestnut Springs everybody said I was drunk. But when I was drinking you couldn't *make* me mad."

The church in my earliest memory looked pretty much the same as it had since the 1870s. Except for the goosenecked electric light on the front there was just the plain narrow chapel at the foot of the mountain with a chickencoop of a steeple. Everybody claimed it had the best sounding bell in the area, a point of pride with the members. In the front were five or six giant Irish junipers making the grounds look funereal from a distance. A half-circle of whitepines my father had planted in the Thirties was beginning to dominate the background.

Just after the clapboard structure was erected the membership split into factions over whether they should buy an organ to accompany the singing. To one branch of the family hymns were to be sung a cappella and the organ was an instrument of the devil. The organ lovers won, but the rift never healed and was aggravated later in the 1890s when some of the winning side began to attend the Holiness revivals held by a passing preacher in a brush arbor.

Essential to the preparations for homecoming was the hauling out of the iron wash-pot to be set on rocks at the south end of the oaks for coffee-making. That job was the responsibility of a distant cousin who had worked in a diner down on the highway during the war. He would bring the firewood in his pickup. It was muttered by various wives and elders that he never came to church otherwise, but each year he was back, standing by the black cauldron steeping a flour sack half-full of grounds in the boiling water. All who dippered out a cup agreed he was an expert.

It was my mother's duty, as it had been her mother's before her, to provide the lemonade. This meant getting a big wooden barrel out of the toolshed a week before and filling it with water to soak and swell the staves tight. I got to pull out the plug that drained it before the lemonade was put in. Two ten-pound bags of sugar dissolved and heated to a syrup, two quarts of lemon juice squeezed by hand, were dumped in and stirred with ice and water for an hour before the cloth was tied over the top to keep out flies. We made it on the tailgate of the truck and drove slowly, clinking, to the church, parking not far from the coffee.

Evangelism struck the community late in the nineteenth century. The first meetings in the brush arbor at Green River were probably attended by my great-grandfather and his daughter out of curiosity. But they came back, participating before long in the shouting, holy-dancing, speaking in tongues. They and maybe a dozen other relatives received the baptism of fire, which lifts the recipient beyond falling from grace. This is specifically contrary to Baptist doctrine which denies falling from grace in the first place. Outraged by the shrieks and crying that came from the arbor late in the summer nights, the more orthodox of the congregation, including those who had earlier opposed buying the organ, held a secret Saturday meeting and after much prayer churched their cousins, the son and grandchildren of the original founder. The families of the community split bitterly, husbands against wives, sisters against sisters-in-law, sons against mothers. But my great-grandfather, who had survived a winter in the Union prison camp at Elmira after capture at Petersburg and returned home still a Republican, an admirer of Lincoln, continued attending services, including prayer meetings and singings, with all his family. He refused to acknowledge or even discuss the excommunication. In time the revivals died away and church affairs went on pretty much as before, at least on the surface. It seemed almost as if the quarrel had been forgotten among the many cornshuckings, poundings for the poor, the intermarrying between the families.

Homecoming Sunday the preaching let out early so the women could unpack baskets and boxes left in backseats and truckbeds. They spread cloths on the weathered lumber of the tables that sagged as trays of fried chicken, each with a different shade of gold or brown and a unique flavor, hams, pickled beans, rice, slaw, biscuits, platters of okra, new potatoes, cornfield beans, coconut cakes, and jugs of iced tea were loaded on. An aunt who specialized in banana puddings always brought a couple of bowls. The church provided paper plates and cups, wooden forks and spoons, cases of ice cream and cones. A few years after the renovations and new wings were added I remember Preacher Brian burning a mortgage note just after grace had been said and before we started eating. He was a heavy Irishman from upper South Carolina who worked as a mechanic weekdays. It had been a good season for the bean farmers and they raised all the money in a rush of zeal before Homecoming. In the bright sunlight the flame Brian put to the note was invisible; all we could see was the paper soaking up blackness and tightening to ashes.

Most of the men stood talking while they ate. A few would rest on bumpers or running boards. Children dashed from section to section of the table grabbing favorite helpings. Women generally stood near the food they had brought brushing away flies. A few tourists would stop by in bermudas and with cameras, and young men who after the war had moved to Greenville or Spartanburg drove up with their families in new cars. There would even be a few people from town, produce buyers, managers of the feed stores, with their families. The young of the community, proud of the money they made picking beans, always overdressed. Once a friend of mine came in the hot August sun wearing an expensive wool hat bought just for the Homecoming.

Quartets and trios converged from other churches up to a hundred miles away. They came for the trip, for the food, and because they loved to sing. Some hoped to make a name for themselves and go professional, like the Blue Ridge Quartet. Older groups traveled around to the little churches where old hymns were sung and shaped notes still legible. I remember men in their seventies, red-faced and mopping brows, leading the singing, calling out antiphonally the next verse to be sung, their shirt sleeves held by garters as they conducted. One quintet from Knoxville was composed of a family of afflicted people. The middleaged daughters were either blind or lame; the son, his frail body contorted in a wheelchair, by polio or arthritis, had an enormous head and wavy red hair. For months after they sang at the church I dreamed of the special tennis shoes he wore.

The next rupture in the membership came in the 1930s when my grandfather on the other side and all his children were turned out by the older conservatives for attending Bible classes taught in the schoolhouse by a self-educated and self-ordained theologian named Metcalfe, called by the locals "Madcaps." Metcalfe's specialty was interpretation of *Revelation.* In my childhood my grandfather still had a mound of pamphlets and tracts he had collected from Metcalfe and radio preachers explaining contemporary events through passages in *Revelation.* They were heaped on top of the china closet and still accumulating. This time the dispute came to a trial, presided over by a county judge and held in the schoolhouse. They won back their membership, but the hostility lingered in the air into my time. During the Depression that grandfather, after four of his children had near-fatal brushes with typhoid, and he could find no work to pay the doctor bills, almost lost his place to the bank. A distant cousin said in church, "I've waited all my life to see that man flat." After the war the son of one of his rivals rose one Sunday to say that in a vision it had been revealed to him my Uncle Robert's death in Europe had been sent as punishment for family sins.

While the singing went on through the afternoon we kids played out among the tables and trees, finishing the lemonade and ice cream with the flies, sailing used paper plates like discuses down toward the spring in the pasture. It was strange to run through the grass in Sunday clothes, watching cows crop among the piles and settling plates same as other days. The mud-caked tires of my uncle's tractor in his yard nearby seemed unusually harsh in the sun's sabbath brightness. The sweaty tractor seat turned up like a short man against dew or rain.

While we littered the grass among the cowpiles with plates, thunderheads crept up over the rim from South Carolina. If rain started before the singing let out, men and children would come dashing outside to roll up car and truck windows, put boxes under canvas or in trunks. Women nursing babies under the pines ran to the cars. After rain it would be cool and the sky clearing as we drove or walked home.

The last break came in the 1950s, just a year after the church was remodeled. Wings had been added for Sunday school classes, and the auditorium lengthened at the back, a vestibule built, and a taller steeple. There was even talk of putting in stained glass, to go with the new pews and pulpit. Perhaps Preacher Brian's lack of diplomacy precipitated the trouble. He had offended many of the conservatives by ignoring several annual meetings of the Southern Baptist Convention. Also he and my father had led a rebellion against using official Baptist literature for Sunday school because it included quotes from the RSV which denied or at least sidestepped the doctrine of the Virgin Birth. The tension was mounting and when it came time to re-elect the preacher at New Year Brian was ousted by a margin of one vote. My father then moved that the church withdraw for good from the Southern Baptist Convention. Over-ruled again by one vote, having chafed for years at this congregation that had expelled his mother as a girl for shouting and speaking in tongues (she died of measles when he was seven), he took the vote as a final insult and walked out never to return. This ended a struggle that began a hundred years before over a foot-pump organ. Exactly half the congregation followed him away. Some joined other churches; one splinter group built a new Pentecostal church just up the creek near the family cemetery. The remaining members threatened to sue Brian for stealing funds intended for buying a small portable organ to carry to home prayer-meetings. He was outraged, but helpless against the rumor that kept him from ever getting another pastorate. Years later he took the job of jailer for the county, and in a scuffle with a prisoner his pistol went off wounding the man in the groin. The prisoner bled to death before the ambulance arrived. Brian was acquitted legally, but again condemned by popular opinion. He moved back to South Carolina to work as a mechanic. Always heavy, and getting fatter, he died of a heart attack within a year.

There was no preaching the night after homecoming. Visitors from town would often come home with us and stay for a light supper of left-overs. If there were children they'd go with me to round up the cows and often stand marveling while I milked. School was only a week away and my sister would bring out the new dresses bought with her own money. There was money all around if it had been a good year for beans. My father would be overly generous to passing evangelists and former pastors, and by October broke again, looking for oddjobs and housepainting.

On my last trip home I saw the church at Green River has been bricked. It is no longer the spare white building at the foot of Meetinghouse Mountain, but a thick structure of dull red. The pines have been cut, and the Irish junipers. All but one of the great oaks have been taken down to expand the parking lot. A baptistry has been added in an annex behind the pulpit with a painting of the river Jordan above it. Stained windows keep the young ones from looking out at the mountains and sky during services.

But the community has changed even more rapidly and drastically. Instead of the small frame houses just getting electricity which I knew as a boy, hundreds of long ranchers have been constructed along the creeks and in shelves cut out of the mountainsides, reflecting the incredible wealth that has followed industry and tourism. Everything seems brand new, the roads, cars, clothes, even mailboxes. Instead of tractors and pickups new sports cars sit in many yards. The Homecomings haven't been held for years, and church attendance fluctuates by season. Even those who still go to preaching take long drives on Sunday afternoons, on the interstates, to Greenville, or Knoxville, and even Charlotte.

PART III

MOCKINGBIRD

While the bee sleeps in the southern night
and weeds weigh under dowries of dew,
above the distant honky-tonk of falls in
the July dark, before the katydids, when
the only frost is lunar, a voice that
raises the hackles on mountains and chills
the barometric spine, that radios through
many channels in the crab orchard and from
maples above the road. What madrigalist
watering the night with polyphony?
You could see orchestras and oratorios
in the polyglot dark, not so much a
mocking of the many-voiced populations
as a gathering to unlikely congregation
of all song, an anthology including
rooster and cricket broadcast from an ounce
of hot flesh through its briar tongue and filling
the hollows and thickets and dry ditches of
the river valley, and soaking under eaves
to the inner ear's accelerator,
circling quick into sleep and bombarding
the ledges of dream.
                    It is my time then;
I surface like the drowned man after three
days and lie trembling with attention to
the heart's perpetual bass. The dark belongs
to me, the peak of alert night. Mama said,
Then is the time to think about God and
feel close to him. But I float in a
sentient medium that amplifies the
distant creek rubbing its rocks, and mist
muddying the weeds by the dusty road,
and I hear the big distance between stars
where two almost light in the oak by the
window. The ascending particle
contraltos. The river's a great liquid
bird singing all day between boulders,

over logs and around bushy islands.
Empties through the gorge its burden without
lessening. All night sings under westering
stars, loudest in the dark before day.
                    And then –
the house barks and pops in far corners
under eaves. The loudest reports are from
dark tin shrinking. Between come squeaks of a
nail growling from its sheath as a corner
settles. And one hard oakboard jams into
a soft piece of pine giving with sharp jolts
and tremors like microseismic quakes of
slippage along a scarp. In damp
weather the distant waterfall sounds close,
brought right to the ear and whispered by
droplets passing the voice on like ions
charging a medium. As if space were a
superconductor heightening all sounds
in a great vowel shift. Night gathers round
its earphones piercing windows in the curtains
so you hear the wail of galaxies and thresh of dust
in canyons of gases, hear the dark
giving birth to stars. Impacts, pings and thuds
from meteorites, splashdown of photons.
Like the music inside a crystal slowly
eaten away. Novas strike and go out.
Sills and cells long forgotten knock and tickle,
tick like boxes hiding their alarms. Even
the genes send out signals, far screams.
Now then, the weeds' pharmacy is damp
and busy along the driplines as a typist's
hammers. The nightingale arias steep
as the terrain and various as the
Geographic. As the hen hatches with
her blotting shadow so ignorance
reveals. Believe in the immaculate
conception of matter from energy.

Wind yodels in the high crevices where
vacuums and near-vacuums vowel its flow.
The dark's a treasure and the mighty skull
of night hurls planetaria. We malinger
where chaos threads and returns like a
windpath across fields. The sea douches
caves and drains the earth's lung. In the windless
dawn snow stands maybe half an inch high on
the fence wires. We hoard our dirt a few
decades while seconds drive pitons of
measure into the jealous mountain. Only
polygraphs reveal time's lie. You will have
the witness of many writings. Coming
up too fast we explode like fish of the
deepest troughs. Stay with high moor and
mountain, the ultraviolet region.
Climb far enough and you reach polar ice
at the equator, get up close to the
bear and dipper. Don't let the mountain's
shadow fall on you like an oilslick, but
as snow on desert canyons, on the
cactus in bloom. Your work will be radical
as the springhead. Start at the beginning
with failure and stand up in the wind. Get
to the bottom and live there, with
land features unaltered by the human.
Work with earthworks, drainages, climates, soils,
find ramparts, embankments, salute agger-making
erosion. Pour footings and drive pilings,
excavate underlying entanglements.
Interpret literally the eros of detail,
the saints of wind and water. Watch the
clear branch twist and mingle with the trash-filled
creek. Audition for the future. Know time as
magnification, as the sun is
amplified by the horizon. Tend
the rocks as a hen turning her clutch of

eggs. Though drought casehardens soil the night
lets down its milk. See entities beyond
nomination, and let words be vouchers
of time put in among the refuse. Feel the
gully's flowcharts and undertows. Up Hominy
the mountain has been lobotomized. Feel
the church's talon in the night sky.
Collaborate with infusoria
to make new each recumbent giant. What
manitous lurk in the hives of trash
washed up after flood? Making light brings
no illumination. Play with matches,
correspondences. Keep the covenant
with bottomlands and shovel down into
the atom's masonry. Like the banyan
send new trunks to root and spread
into a grove. From the fenlands watch the
mountain's gargoyles. You have spoken.
Now then the accent varies, and from
the flats along the creek in still loftier
cleft that mirrors hawk and partridge. Don't try
to filibuster nature. The art of culture
is always substitution. The knife must
turn to keep its honey. Note nature's
formality and the million intersections
in a piece of cloth. Slice the terrain in
strips evading fungus and depletion, and
play them like bands of the spectrum.
Recombination captures more of sunlight
and mineral. People on mountaintops
age slower, says Einstein. The clock's heart
knocks in its cabinet. Think of vegetal
glass and optical flesh. Though time's a
potentate and clay a tyrant, the law
of conservation means the world's
an anagram of each stage of evolution.
Come red shift in stellar wind, flow sweet as
the milk of new corn.

And the bird outside parodically
now mocking the encyclic dream. The
mountains will not give way and flood us with
the emptiness they hold back all the way to
stars. The sky will maintain its arched
integrity like a hogan roof. Matter
will not burst out of itself without
provocation, critical accumulation.
The dam will not fail with fatigue but feed
evenly through its spillway. History
impounded above the settlements is stable.
Failure's a kind of dam holding back while
we work the bedrock, fool around in the
valley before shooting the rapids. The
orison high as thermometer's blood.
August the creek goes rabid and froths at
the slightest ripple, builds a head on the
backwater whipping a tough meringue
below the falls going out an eye
at a time. Drools through sticks at the foot
of the pool. The suds wither gummy,
a skim the minnows suck at.

And now from the steep lawn of pasture
hill a chant more light than voice, many-tongued,
rising through miles of rock and soil. See
lifting deep in the strata to newplowed fields
and under rivers the faraway beginning
of your own resurrection, a heat
moving toward its source. Somewhere your fall
and its rising will coincide as a
missile intercepted by its shadow. Now
it already pursues in a future-seeking
trajectory and whether you turn aside
or run it rises there below the surface
coming steadily on toward the point
of contact and cannot be shaken. As

the reflection of a skydiver thrown
on a far hill rushes to meet its source
at impact, it draws you to its flash.
Every hour contains ice ages, every
second all of evolution. A
single bee whines in the glass hive of the
electric meter where a turntable
plays its recording of power, where the
watt and kilowatt accumulate like
cells of honey. Here multiple wires
feed the clear nipple. The ticker comes in
unseen but counted as the calories of the lake
falling out of itself tally and the
hidden current turrets and the bubble
inflates with electrons. The house
drinks from its tipped jar. Now through
repeating cycles the species stands idling
for a few yugas when out of some distant
nothing a particle, weightless and
chargeless, scores on the chromosome gearbox
shuffling and reengaging the serrated
coins. Without helmsman the thing careers
away onto rocks, over gullies, cliffs,
frottaging trees into the mire, or like a
tortoise stays flipped on its back until
unfueled. Maybe one out of a million
finds a negotiable course, arrives to slip
out of gear again and then idle for
ages in a congenial spot on
higher more defensible ground.

Now then who sings from deep under, beneath
subfloor, sill, and cellar, below foundations,
an artesian voice issuing out of the
crevices to its own stellar level,
slipping from branch to frond in the kelp
forest where bellropes and long tongues

stir in the slightest current, each leaf
containing more chlorophyll than
sequoias, big and sleepy as dinosaurs.
The biggest deserts on the earth lie
underneath. There currents from the poles
howl down slopes onto the abyssal plain
and roll through canyons never still. Above
fish blow against the ledges like leaves and
butterflies in thermals, flash away like
seeds from maples. And always on the slopes the
planktonic snow settles quietly and loads
the walls until they fail in cloudy slides
that fill the valleys with dust blizzards for
weeks and tear the buried cables. Boulders
rafted from the arctic in ice bomb the
trenches and freezing rivers scour tracks of
stilted swimmers, tripod fish, and plowmarks
of giant worms. In mineral gardens the
charged sea plates rocky nodules slowly.
Bushel snails skim the ooze like cream.
Gullies empty silt aprons in bins where tides
winnow the trash of continents. Far up in
the mountains a sandfall carves icy time
where once a pasture heaved its wet grass at
the moon.

I will be what I will be. It is the
dead speaking now from every petal
of the compass, every atom in
the dark traffic. The voice ascends at the
wavelength of mountains out of the swamp musk
into the crypt of sky, builds loglog concision
in the night of Babylonian weight,
a table whose bulbed legs whirl gyroscopically
vertical, with grain distinct as the
thumbprint of a file or the ingots of
a snake's belly. Say the statute of

limitations has run out on original
sin, take quiddity of tumbleweed, the
medicine river, take fernbrakes and a
mouse gnawing the Atlantic cable to
swill electrons, take rawhide and Cherokees,
the county seat and demonology,
take the stream going underground in late
summer leaving puddles of fry thickening
among white rocks. Take the hotair
balloon lifted by the tongue's candle, take
the sermon as firedrill, take hold of
badlands and dismantle the earth's spinning
integrity for an exploded view. It's
difficult to leave the country where your
ancestors are buried. Take colander
and breeding pond, a sapling with its wrists
cut. Climbing down the tree of Porphyry,
getting it right most when switching and
vacillating. Going east to arrive
west. Walk backwards in the snow leaving
tracks that arrive where they originate
and leave where they are going. Parabolic
sayings augment the ministry of rushes.
Through hatred eat the midden manna. Let
disinclinations affirm, improvise
a testament, masseur of mud. Seated
wherever speak ex cathedra. Be a
pallbearer of seed into dirt and bear
with solemnity and care the husk of
the ideal to its grave. Shatter the
perfect orbits of atoms to refind
the light buried there. Where is the man who
would not kill to be reborn? I have heard
the pain of the mountain dulcimer
across the cove. Follow the smallest stream
to its cliffs and cross over to the knob
country and the defile to the west, stand

in the electrolytic dark and feel
the creek lick over rocks. Even though you
turn back and circumnavigate do not
turn back. Do not be struck with stagefright on
the summit. Know the buck holds his head
erect when he runs and the doe waves.
Licensed to plead for yourself in
history bear to citydump and fertilizer
plant the thermal waste and bilge of learning.
Dive beneath the thermocline and come up
like a pale sprout from the darkroom.
Unable to find a parking place in
the city don't panic. You are one gene
in the cells of the body of language.
Go fast awake through the laurel slicks, the
electric blanket of foliage. Since
nobody understands more than a fraction
at a time it's good to keep records. Don't
confidence theory. Carry these sayings
to the south breeze, to the dirt's craw, the
ground spewed up with frost. Create brief
Yoknapatawphas, a potlatch of words.
Climb through the thickets of Big Hungry
AWOL from society. Take bat's milk, the
eagle's seed, and sleep in coral underbrush.
Each rock and bit of trash is an avatar
and mud hardening to crust a voice.
The virtual coil of dust is erotic.
Thirsty ventricles gulp and swallow.
Mountains speak in tongues. Take the wide thought
of estuaries. The absent god leaves the forest
and tundra soaked in divinity. In
Egyptian silence, trappist restraint, hear
thunder. Being is fed by time as by
oxygen. Swampwater's black as a new
Cadillac. Take Saluda River and
Shoestring Creek and Bullpen Gap. Don't cringe at

the thought of Grandma with her birch toothbrush
and the sullen sentiment of isolated
coves. Take the timbered-off slopes and the
stumphouse on Eyelet Ridge. Build with undressed
stone. An illiterate ancestor won the
battle of Cowpens. Reject the dryhides and
take the holy dance. Take the land beyond
the fall-line, beyond the corduroy road
and depot, and ford the creek lengthwise to
get into town. Offer reticence and disapprobation,
follow no trade, and heading for deep cover
come to an opening in the canopy
where light shines from obscure places. Hide
behind a waterfall in congregation
with mist and rock. Take the justified
margin of cornfields. Inaugurate by
leaving, ordained by anonymity.

Robert Morgan is the author of several books of poems, including *Terroir* (2011) and *Dark Energy* (2015). He has published twelve books of fiction, including *The New York Times* bestseller *Gap Creek*, and, most recently, *Chasing the North Star* (2016), *As Rain Turns to Snow* (2017), and *In the Snowbird Mountains and Other Stories* (2023). His works of nonfiction include *Lions of the West* (2011), *Fallen Angel: The Life of Edgar Allan Poe* (2023), and the national bestseller *Boone: A Biography* (2007). Recipient of awards from the Guggenheim Foundation and the American Academy of Arts and Letters, he is currently Kappa Alpha Professor of English (Emeritus) at Cornell University.